Good Horses
Make
Good Jockeys

D1429058

Good Horses Make Good Jockeys

RICHARD PITMAN

PELHAM BOOKS

First published in Great Britain by Pelham Books Ltd
52 Bedford Square, London WC1B 3EF
1976

ISBN 0 7207 0911 3

Set and printed in Great Britain by
Tonbridge Printers Ltd, Tonbridge, Kent,
in Garamond eleven on thirteen point,
on paper supplied by P. F. Bingham Ltd,
and bound by Redwood Burn, at Esher, Surrey

Contents

Illustrations

27. Killiney jumps high over the open ditch at Cheltenham.

28. I could always be recognised by my thighs.

29. Jumping Bechers Brook.

Between pages 92–93

30. Pendil (No. 4) takes the open ditch for the last time before going on to win the King George VI Chase at Kempton in 1973.

31. A great horse – the head of Killiney.

32. Another great horse – Crisp at the Parade of Champions, Wembley, 1975.

33. Taking a bend.

34. Pendil studies his own reflection in the water jump at Kempton Park.

35. You can see here why Gerry Cranham labelled me a floating jockey.

36. The photo-finish to the 1973 Cheltenham Gold Cup, with The Dikler taking Pendil by a short head.

37. Teaching a two-year-old to jump.

38. The 1973 Grand National. Crisp clears the Canal Turn well in front of the field.

39. The 1973 Grand National. The end of a *great* race.

40. My biggest disappointment – no – the thrill of my life.

41. Our first racehorse.

42. Larbawn on holiday, being ridden by Eric Wheeler.

43. 'What's happening over there then?' Paul's bribes are rejected!

44. A man of leisure!

45. Contentment.

1 *The why, how and when*

I remember how I pressed myself tight against the wing of the fence, halfway down the hill at Cheltenham where I had crept in over the railway line an hour before the first race—the place I found every time that I played truant from school.

The seven runners topped the crest of the hill and surged towards my fence, the noise increasing with every stride. Packed tightly together, they rose as one; birch flew into the air; the grey, bellying the fence, grunted as the wind was knocked out of him. A shout came from one jockey, and a curse from another. There was a thud as the horses landed, then a cracking of whips—the spoils were in sight—and then, the noise fading, the moving shapes on a wedge of green grass disappeared amongst the mass of colour made up of the paying public.

To a boy, now standing alone half a mile away, the distant crowd might have been a garden party at Buckingham Palace. I had been a non-paying, unwanted witness to a steeplechase at Cheltenham. But I was drawn to this spectacle which was already like a drug to me. I needed more, I waited half an hour before the next race. My parents would be angry, the headmaster would see through my forged sickness note the next day, but no price was too high. I would stay there—little knowing that that very fence was to play a vital part in my undoing in the 1974 Gold Cup. Indeed if it had been suggested then that I would ever gallop down that slope I would have laughed.

Despite my doubts, my sister Pam was determined to make a rider of me. She made me rise at 6 a.m., cycle three miles to the foot of Cleeve Hill and endeavour to catch Honeybunch, an elderly piebald pony who had seen many such enthusiasts during his fourteen years. He loved to evade a would-be rider but would finally tire of this game and stop for his head to be put into the bridle.

Pam would cycle beside me, attached by a rope. When Honeybunch heard the gentle order 'Prepare to trot' he obediently trotted. Every morning for a week I had baled out from the saddle when the 'Prepare to canter' reached Honeybunch's ears. The trot was safe enough but the canter was unknown territory. If Pam had not pushed me through that particular barrier, I might never have been a jockey. (Reading this many punters will no doubt shower curses on her.) One day she omitted the verbal instruction and instead, gave Honeybunch a sharp smack on the rump—and I found myself enjoying my first canter.

Despite the discovery that I enjoyed riding—and riding fast—I only became a jockey because of failing my 'O' levels.

I was educated at Tewkesbury Grammar School, a manor house set in parkland with beautiful views on all sides. Whenever I could, during my six-year stay there, I managed to get a seat in the large bay window which was a feature of each classroom, and sat and day-dreamed. As the master asked 'What was I saying Pitman?' I was watching myself sitting by the 'Washpool' an hour's ride over the Cleeve Hill, with occasional cows and sheep intruding into the valley to drink the cool spring water. I was indeed an outdoor boy, but I seemed destined to follow my father's footsteps as an aircraft instrument engineer. The previous year I had sat and passed eight subjects in the mock school certificate examination, border line on a ninth. Now I was sitting the GCE 'O' level exams in nine subjects. I completed each examination in good time; they seemed not too hard. With a bit of luck I would pass all nine; at the worst I ought to pass seven.

The results came in the post during the holidays. I tore open the envelope and there against each subject was a large 'F'. I could scarcely believe that it stood for 'Failed'. My father was furious and did not speak to me for several days. I had let him down badly.

Looking back, it would be nice to think that I had failed on purpose so that I could follow my chosen profession; but of course this was not so.

All the same, my exam failure opened the way. Pam was courting Paddy Cowley who had just come over from Ireland to ride for Phil Doherty. After a short trial with Mr Doherty I joined his staff in 1959. I look back with a shudder to think what a sight I must have been when I joined: a small boy with masses of freckles and crew-cut hair, wearing a rust-coloured polo-necked jumper, old jeans and a large pair of farming gum-boots. I looked like an otter-hound when I should have been like a smooth-haired terrier, alert, cocky, smart in appearance, loud enough to be noticed without being too yappy. In a small stable you have time to change for the better. But if he enters a large trainer's yard lacking these qualities, or something like them, a would-be jockey is liable to be defeated by weight of numbers. If the opportunity is not seized quickly, younger and brighter sparks overtake and the hopefuls fade into the structure of the stable.

My story was the exception to the rule. I wandered winner-less for four years and rode twenty-two winners during the next three years: after seven years as a professional jockey my average was three victories a year. I scarcely set the world alight—but, like the tortoise, I arrived eventually. You need friends to help you when you begin a career like that. If I do not have the space to thank all those early friends, it is not because I have forgotten them.

My job with Phil Doherty had only lasted six months when his licence was withdrawn for having dope found in one of his horses. Although I was young at the time, I was sure then and have remained convinced that he was innocent of the charge. The horse in question was called Precipite, an ex-tremely strong animal who was running for the first time in eighteen months. He sweated up badly in the paddock and pushed me into the rails on several occasions, drawing conspicious attention to himself. He started at long odds and duly pulled up in the race. The drug found was a stimulant. Had it been administered for a coup the horse would surely have been backed heavily, but the price was 20–1—a reasonable price for a horse that had not run for such a long while.

The enquiry was held at the old National Hunt Committee offices in Cavendish Square. We, the accused party and his witnesses were bundled into a small cloakroom without a window under the stairs; an electric light shone brightly and there was an old tobacco tin for an ash tray. For me, a small boy who had never been to London before, it created visions of cells below and bread and water. At last I was called. I was led down endless corridors until we came to a halt before a pair of impressive double doors reaching up to a high ceiling. These were opened and I was pushed gently into the room.

Sitting at the far end were five very stern-looking men. The eldest (and grumpiest) beckoned me to him and with each step echoing around the room I cautiously advanced. My stay was brief and was conducted rather as I imagine a Court Martial. Phil was found guilty of being the trainer in charge of a doped horse, although not blamed personally. At that time guilt, even on this technical charge, meant automatic dismissal from the ranks of the trainers. This unnecessarily harsh rule was changed some years later to a fine of £100. Outside the building Phil broke down and cried. His trade had been taken from him. Training was the only thing that he knew, a trade of which he was a master. For Phil Doherty was a first-class trainer of second-class horses, and this was a blow which he never recovered from.

So, scarcely had I begun but I was out of a job, along with Phil, and had to look for another. Having scanned *Horses in Training* I selected Major Geoffrey Champneys at Upper Lambourn as the next employer I wanted to work for. Obviously I needed a few knocks yet before my feet were planted firmly on the ground, but surely everyone sets out with delusions of grandeur? I remain deeply indebted to the Major and, if he is still training when my sons are old enough, I could wish for no better man to finish their education. He is a gentleman, absolutely honest and an example to all men. I was a terrible nuisance to him: every day I would ask the same question 'Will you get me a Jockey's Licence, please sir?' only to get the same reply 'No, not this week Pip'. He relented after several months and took out a jockey's licence for me just to keep me quiet.

Like the door-to-door salesman who lands a sale I was back the next day for more. This time the plea was 'Will you have a ride for me in public, please sir?'

In the end, the Major gave me five rides that season, two of which had chances of winning.

The first, Pasadena, was favourite, but she broke a blood vessel and trailed in last of the five runners. As I trotted back past the stands to the paddock I was greeted by jeers. One particularly obscene punter made me so angry that I pulled my stick through and hit him on top of his head. I felt much better for I knew that having had a dose himself he would no longer shout for a jockey to hit the horse that was carrying his wager. My relief was short-lived. An official beckoned me to the steward's room. I was told I was the most insignificant object on the racecourse that day and I should realise that the punter with the lump on his head indirectly paid my wages: furthermore it was his prerogative to hint that I was of doubtful parentage.

My second fancied ride was at Fontwell Park on Whit Monday. Coming round the last bend in second place, I saw that the leader was not going at all well so I moved up to him, ready to go on to win when I chose. The experienced jockey on the leader picked up his whip as I drew almost level and hit my poor horse four times across the head. Not understanding or approving of this violent action, my horse dropped the bit; as a result I sat down with a bump and dropped my whip. By the time we recovered our senses the leader had drawn clear and, try as we may, the winning post came just too soon for us to catch him. The Major, thinking I had made a big enough fool of myself already would not let me object, so my second chance was gone.

I should say that I only experienced two more acts of foul riding of that kind in the fifteen years I rode; and it is satisfying to know that it never did the guilty parties any lasting good: all three turned out to be lacking real guts and eventually racing had no place for them.

2 Growing up in the racing industry

Working for Major Champneys took me away from home for the first time. This was my early step towards manhood and, of course, drinking was included in the curriculum. Every night my buddy Wally Walpole and I would walk the mile to the Malt Shovel, make two halves of cider last all night and sing our way back to bed. We fought bulls, crossed enemy territory, parachuted from the sky and of course, rode many many winners. We were a pair of dreamers.

I always thought Wally was too soft to make a jump jockey, but he proved to me that he was made of stronger stuff than I could ever be. One night as we were coming home from a victory party given by Bryan Marshall I decided to put Wally to the test. We were travelling on my moped, Wally seated on the parcel rack. When I started to ride with no hands he complained, but too late. The front wheel hit a stone and moped, Wally and I hit the floor. The skin was torn from the top of my head to my waist and Wally could not move his arm. We both crept home to our respective digs to lick our wounds. Three days later he was still in bed unseen by the doctor because he did not want to get a friend into trouble. The doctor, when summoned, diagnosed a broken shoulder and whisked him off to hospital. I have not known many better acts of friendship.

The fact that I now earned a living prompted me to do the things that you have to do yourself to discover that they really are mugs games—for example playing cards and having too much to drink. It is not until you wake up with a throbbing head and no wages in your pocket that you realise the things Mother told you before leaving home were right. These silly phases soon passed; and appreciating home so much more than when I lived there, I asked the Major if I could go back to Cheltenham. He was probably pleased: I was still too big for my boots, and tiresome with my continual request for rides.

I left one Friday evening indebted to the Major for teaching me self respect, pride in my work and myself and a thorough grounding in stable work. As I walked across the yard he shouted, 'Good luck Pip. Let me know how you get on,' to which I replied, 'Just read the *Sporting Life* Major. You can read all about me there.' (It was a few years before I appeared in print and then the report of a race at Plumpton read, 'With all due respect to the rider of the second David Mould outrode him from the last'. That report was correct then and would be correct if we met now: David is an artist, beautiful to watch and extremely effective.) We parted company amicably and I left Lambourn for the first time, but I was destined to return still looking for the end of the rainbow.

At that time Wally and I were escorting the two prettiest girls in the village and for several months I returned on my moped on Sundays to see my girl-friend. One rainy Sunday after my forty-five mile trek against strong headwinds I arrived twenty minutes late, to find my lovely Rita as angry as the storm-clouds above us. Like most women she would not listen to my excuses so I decided that I could get a 'bollocking' forty-five miles nearer home. Both Wally's girl-friend and mine married locally, although I am sure they are eternally thankful that it was not to jockeys.

I learnt a lot at this time from the blacksmith Vic Alderton who would pass on to me the benefit of his seventy-five years. When I told him of my love troubles he said, 'Son, there are many girls you could live with. You find the one you can't live without.' It was not long before I learnt what he meant.

After a short spell with A. A. Gilbert near Cheltenham, I went to work for John Roberts at Prestbury in 1961. The moped seized up and was replaced by a bicycle, and Lambourn was behind me. Was I a failure? At the time I thought of this as just a lull in proceedings. I must have had an enlarged opinion of myself to keep me oblivious of the truth: I was going nowhere fast. I was going fast though, one day, coming round a bend on my bike, nearly colliding with a string of racehorses lead by a beautiful young blonde girl who gave me the rough end of her tongue. I was right about getting the treatment at home!

I next saw that girl having a drink with a lad in a pub in Cheltenham. When throwing out time came round, we saw to our delight that it had snowed heavily. This providing an excuse for Jenny and me to slip over, grabbing at each other, we finally came to rest with our lips touching. That was that. The lad escorting Jenny bowed out gracefully.

3 You'll never be a champion jockey but you'll do

I spent two happy seasons with John Roberts. He was a very nice man, in fact too nice for this egotistic young jockey; what I really needed was someone to kick my backside until they made contact with my brains. John gave me all the rides he could and secured many outside rides for local permit holders and his old friends. During the next two years I gained a lot of experience but never looked like riding a winner. As most young jockeys do, I rode with too short a stirrup and could not slip rein when the horse needed his head. I learnt to slip rein one afternoon at Chepstow when both Peter Graham and Hardy had unseated me in full view of the stands. Both horses pulled me over their heads because I could not give them the rein they needed. Something had to give and horse being stronger than man it was I who flew through the air with the greatest of ease.

About this time I found much to my amazement that Jenny was receiving romantic letters from one of 'Frenchie' Nicholson's apprentices. Our respective strings of horses passed and to my delight I saw that my opposition was small, ginger-haired and only about five stones wet through. I shouted that I wanted to see him sometime and I was astonished when I left the stables for lunch to be confronted by this midget. His face was slightly flushed, but he gave nothing else away. This fighting cock, no, more a bantam, used the old weapon of surprise : facing each other we burst out laughing.

Paul Cook was to be Frenchie's first really successful apprentice jockey; he had shown at that early age the strength of his character. He is a quiet, unassuming, jockey but is ready to back up his convictions. And he has shown the racing world his metal. After a brilliantly successful apprenticeship Paul fell out of favour, but through hard work, determination, together with his natural ability, he has fought his way back amongst the top jockeys where he belongs.

John Roberts' health was not very good so his string was getting smaller and I decided to look around for my fifth job in racing. It was an arduous task for I decided to go through every one of the trainers listed in *Horses in Training*, seeing who they employed as First Jockey and what lads they had as prospects. Each major trainer had a long list of lads with licenses. After scratching my head for a week (probably why my hair is so thin) I decided to follow the advice of Leslie, the horsebox driver. Leslie lived in Oddington, near Stow-on-the-Wold. Fred Winter, who also lived there, had told him that he might retire from riding a year thence. I wrote to Mr Winter, who was my boyhood hero and to whom I had never dared to speak, although I had ridden in many races with him.

He had earned the inside berth at the start of a race. If a young jockey had got there first a cold piercing stare would be enough to make the intruder move out, leaving the space for the master. His reply to my letter was encouraging; he would watch me ride at Cheltenham the following month and see if I had any ability at all. The big day came round. Mr Winter made no attempt to speak to me and I thought that the small matter of my future had slipped his memory. But after the race, in which I did nothing outstanding, but also nothing wrong, he approached me and said, 'You'll never be champion jockey but you'll do.' He was, of course, correct: I was twice second in the championship – and I did!

Three weeks after my interview with Fred Winter I saw just why he was a champion rider. It was at Leicester. Fred Winter was riding Carry On, one of three runners in a chase, at the prohibitive odds of 3–1 on. The result looked a foregone conclusion, but at the ninth fence, to the dismay of the crowd, the favourite fell. They say only fools remount in a steeple-chase. Fred Winter has never been a fool. He remounted quickly and set off in pursuit of the diminishing runners. The surprises were not yet over. Not too pleased by events, Carry On decided that enough was enough, and dug his toes in at the tenth. That was a mistake on his part for now pride was at stake. When asked to try the fence again he realised Fred meant business and that it would be wiser to answer his rider's calls. The other two runners were now some way ahead, but, unhurried, Carry On slowly decreased the gap.

The bookies—experienced race readers—were shouting '4-1 the favourite'—but bringing his mount with a well-timed run, Fred Winter got up after the last fence to win 'cleverly'.

I also particularly remember my new guv'nor win on Madame Hennessy's Mandarin in the French Grand National in a truly magnificent piece of riding. Mandarin's bit broke with a mile and a half to go, leaving Fred Winter with no reins to guide his horse. That race is part of history, but anyone who witnessed it will never forget how he steered his horse with sheer strength of legs and body, and how he kept Mandarin going throughout the driving finish. Fred Winter had shown the world that day, that he had a burning will to win and the ability to back it up.

I took my place in the weighing room when it was full of genuine characters who really enjoyed riding and living. There was 'Tumper' (Johnny Lehane), a tousle-haired Irish jockey who was generous to a fault. He rode many successful gambles for Bill Marshall's stable and had a lot of money coming in. He delighted in buying drinks for everybody in the local whether he knew them or not. He would give toys to children in the street and presents to older people, not to impress but because he loved life. He had friends in every part of the country and would stay a short while with each, leaving behind him enough clothes to kit three men and next time around those clothes would be washed, aired and ready for him to wear. Johnny loved people and people loved Johnny.

Then there was 'Poacher' (Peter Pickford) a brilliant jockey who invariably poached someone else's ground in a race. He was always fighting his weight and did not get the recognition he deserved, but if Peter really fancied his mount, it won. 'Buller and Heifer' were Josh and Macer Gifford who need no introduction. There was also 'The Brown Cow' Tim Brookshaw, a great horseman; he was without fear throughout his distinguished career and helped young riders to improve whenever needed. His nickname came from his habit of saying— 'How now brown cow'. A lot of stuffed shirts and fancy ladies (or ladies who fancied themselves) may have taken offence at this greeting but none was ever meant and real blue bloods accepted it in the spirit that it was given!

Terry Biddlecombe, although about my age, was a man in racing terms and I a boy, he introduced me to champagne and showed me how to escape from the strains of being a steeplechase jockey. I never ever saw Terry lose his temper in a game where tempers run high. His ever-present smile and mop of blond hair made him everybody's darling, and rightly so. Paddy Cowley was called 'Cowboy' because he often held the back of the saddle with one hand just like a rodeo rider when landing over a jump. There were many such friends and rivals. Most of them left their clothes where they fell when changing before a race, but a shining example to all was Bill Rees who earned the title of 'The Sporting Parson' by his impeccable manners, tidiness of character and non-participation in the vices. To me the weighing room was a magical place.

4　*It's uphill all the way*

In the June of 1964 I entered Lambourn for the second time, still in search of fame and fortune. This time the stables I joined were Uplands. Fred Winter had only six horses and three lads. The head lad was Tommy Carey, an experienced man in all aspects of the game. Alongside him he had Brian Delaney, who three years later became the Guv'nor's right hand, and myself. We three were totally different in every way. Tommy was a real Walter Mitty. He relived the most amazing experiences, and was either a brilliant actor or actually believed his own tall stories. At feed time when he produced a much used pen-knife he might say, 'Laddie, I killed three soldiers with just my bare hands and *this*, one night in an ammo dump in Germany,' and with a quick flick, the shining blade would halve the carrot he held in his hand. My mouth would drop open with admiration, but Brian Delaney, whose army career had been cut short by an ulcer, would raise his eyebrows in disbelief. He knew that the knife most used in the forces was that which peeled the spuds during a session of jankers.

Tommy had tales for every occasion, the 'long tom' he carried, the boots he wore and the scars about his person. He had also invented the canned food industry, helped MGM films out of financial disaster, cultivated ground that had been jungle since time began, and discovered a new breed of oat! Tommy was a character who will be sadly missed. His favourite saying was 'I've told Fred and I won't teach him much more.' In a strange way he was right. Looking back, the Guv'nor has followed the same policy right through his career: to hire the best outsiders until he had modelled his own creations on people and things that had stood the test of time. Tommy was the first head man, but although he had a vast knowledge he could not change at the same pace as this expanding stable and all through those early years, the Guv'nor and Brian Delaney were sifting the useful from the outdated.

The knowledge earned from a lifetime's experience can be bought and paid for relatively quickly: Brian became Fred Winter's next and probably last head man. The same pattern was followed with jockeys. Until he had cultivated a squad of jockeys of his own Fred Winter used established riders for some years: Willie Robinson, Dave Dick, Stan Mellor, Mick Scudamore, Bobby Beasley and Eddie Harty were used in the first season, Eddie gaining favour towards the end and securing the job as first jockey for the next season. Many more top-class riders were employed until the day when Fred Winter's own lads met all his needs. In 1974 I was first jockey, John Francome second, Vic Soane third and two youngsters filled the gaps as claiming jockeys (Robert Kington and Jimmy Guest). Now that I myself have retired everyone moves up one place and also several young hopefuls will get a licence to ride.

We three, Fred Winter's first employees, made an interesting comparison. Where as I have said, Tommy lived in the past, Brian certainly did not and although he did not set out to be Fred Winter's head lad he was certainly looking for a niche higher up the ladder than the one he then held. Brian came from a family which excelled in equine knowledge and he became himself a first-rate jockey, once beating Stan Mellor in a tight finish at Worcester—a fact that he has reminded me of constantly for the last ten years—though he had by then ceased race-riding. From the first, whenever he opened his mouth he said something sensible. His work was of the highest standard and his dress immaculate; when you are shifting dung, strapping horses and getting soaking wet most days in the winter, that is quite hard to maintain. Now that I am older I know that a proper routine is essential. So many youngsters try to cut corners, without realising that they are making a rod for their own back. Brian remains a model in that respect. I was the third man. I had for many years lived with my head amongst the clouds, and although I was in the process of coming down to earth, I had not as yet planted my feet properly on the ground.

After six weeks of trotting on the roads, the morning planned for the string's first canter arrived. The gallops being still hard, Fred Winter decided to canter on the ploughed strip. He rode the hardest puller, much to everyone's delight: an Irish chaser called One Seven Seven. Tommy Carey rode a beautiful grey with impeccable manners, Brian a nice horse called Givenaway, and I rode the oldest inhabitant, a point-to-pointer called Quintina. In that order we were to canter twice around the ploughed strip, well spaced out because of the dust, and at a very steady pace. All was well for one circuit. The Guv'nor up front had a minor argument with One Seven Seven as to the correct speed to canter, but of course won in the end. The rest of us were nicely spaced out and were all trying to put on our neatest style. The only witnesses were a flock of sheep grazing nearby, who were certainly not impressed.

Going out for the second circuit Quintina decided she knew all there was to know about the Lambourn Downs and now really took hold of the bit. I fought her for a while but I was the first to weaken and gradually I got closer to Brian than was comfortable with so much dust being kicked up. A few seconds later I was passing him.

'Pull up you bloody fool,' he shouted, but my arms were now useless. Tommy sat bolt upright when I appeared at his girths and gave the encouragement that I needed: 'I'll skin you laddie!'

My mind was willing but my flesh was weak. Now the boss was in sight and, because I was sweating, the dust was sticking to my face. Hardly able to breathe I sailed past him to win my first race—but there was no 10 per cent of the winnings.

The mare now tired herself, eased to a trot and finally put

her head down to graze. I did not have the strength to pull her up. Slumped in the saddle, dirty, breathless and bearing no resemblance to a jockey, I waited for the master to explode. Perhaps he didn't think me worthy of a rocket; perhaps words could not describe his thoughts; or maybe he just felt sorry for this miserable article, but without a glance at me he led the others past me and on home.

My thoughts on that half hour journey back to the stables can be imagined. How far had the incident ruined my chances of success, or put me back. I was to echo those same questions many times before the job as first jockey to Fred Winter was offered seven years later, and then I could not take it because I was contracted to ride for Major Verly Bewicke. We three were definitely chips from different blocks.

At that time the head man lived in the bungalow at the entrance to the driveway and we lived in a caravan. Quite rapidly the number of horses increased and proportionately the lads did too. Tommy Maguire came as travelling head man, Derrick King to 'do his two', Gloucester Soane and Red Weaver, hopeful jockeys like myself and Bowbells, a chirpy young cockney and so we gathered strength. Caravan life was quite exciting to begin with, but then we were young. Mrs Carey cooked for us in her bungalow and used a wheelbarrow to transport the hot containers of excellent food to our increasing circle of dwellings.

Brian Delaney was the self-elected chief Romany and so prepared a rota for the emptying of the portable loos. I well remember that force was never permitted to persuade another person to take your turn, but payment was! Red Weaver, being quite affluent, started the trend that set one lad on his way to his first million and proved the old Yorkshire saying 'Where there's muck there's brass.'

Tommy Maguire entertained us periodically by falling asleep with a cigarette in his mouth, thus catching the lace curtains and sheets alight or, failing that, he would awake with a yell as the glowing end touched his lips. Some people need a lullaby, Tommy needed his smoke. 'Bowbells' as we called him was very small, but had a huge pair of hands, knees and a boomps a daisy, his ears stuck out at right angles and his face always carried a large smile. He never made a jockey, but eventually the remainder of his body caught up with his larger features and he left racing, we missed him.

The Guv'nor had now to decide whether to put up more stables or to erect a hostel. He did the latter, and soon we were moving into a brand new centrally-heated hostel. It was then and still is his policy to treat his staff as he would like them to treat him, with respect.

Three of us wanted rides and keen competition soon crept in, all of us trying to prove that he was the one to ride Fred Winter's horses to victory. Red polished his boots as if he had done his National Service, so we copied him and everybody's boots shone brightly. Derrick King started work early so that his horses and stables looked immaculate. I carried on, but just to let the Guv'nor know I was keen I would whistle as I walked under his bedroom window at 6.30 a.m. It worked, though not as I planned. He knew who it was because after a week the windows were thrown open and I was lambasted for waking Mrs Winter up at that unearthly hour! Gloucester Soane was like Bowbells, younger, smaller and so at that time, no danger in the race for Fred Winter's favours. He is today not only one of the nicest fellows I know, but also a first-rate jockey, good enough to ride for anyone.

The horses were getting fitter and Red and myself were schooling several of them. We both hoped for that first ride, but who would have it. One evening, as the time for the Guv'nor to look round the horses approached, a car drew up and out jumped one of my owners (rather he owned a horse that I looked after) so to impress I 'borrowed' one of Red's head-collars and polished the brass buckles. I was spotted and asked to give it back. I replied in a short tempered way. This of course, made Red see red and, adopting a stance like an old-fashioned boxer, asked me to apologise or defend myself!

I had never been in a fight in my life, but not wanting to appear yellow in front of Red I adopted a similar stance. I saw it coming, but could not move and so after a searing pain and a blinding flash, I crashed to the floor and there sitting on the wet tarmac I decided that Red could certainly have his head-collar back. The Guv'nor and my owner came into sight at that same time and to our embarrassment led us both by our ears around his house and on to the lawn where we were told to sort out our differences like men, so we shook hands and parted friends.

The American amateur Tommy Smith had swelled our ranks and brought with him Jay Trump, a horse which had twice won the Maryland Hunt Cup, a race over fixed timber. He was to be aimed at the Grand National, and was also going to be Fred Winter's first runner as a trainer, together with One Seven Seven at Ludlow, a secondary meeting. I was delighted and very surprised to be told one evening that Sir Michael Sobell had agreed to let me ride One Seven Seven at Ludlow in a handicap chase. The Guv'nor would be at Sandown and as Sir Michael would not be present no great pressure would be on me.

'Just enjoy yourself and win,' were Fred Winter's last instructions. You can imagine my thoughts as I drove to Ludlow. Had my battle to climb the ladder of success at last paid dividends? The horse was favourite, fit, and should win comfortably, and in fact if we did not win it would surely be because of a mistake on my part. Quickly I dismissed the last thought. This was to be my moment, I must not lose my head.

Brian Delaney looked after Jay Trump and they had left early that morning for Sandown Park, but as far as I was concerned Ludlow was where the action was. I walked the course even though I had ridden there six or seven times before. It helped to occupy my mind which by this time had covered every eventuality from winning easily and looking pretty, too—perhaps I did not really think of it—falling off at the first.

Certainly the fact that I was riding for Fred Winter did make me walk taller. The preliminaries over with, we cantered down to the start. We gathered speed as we went and I was pretty well out of control when the inspection fence loomed up. Being an old hand at the racing game. One Seven Seven dropped his bit and pulled up, just as it looked as if we would collide with the other runners grouped by the fence. It occurred to me that if I could not hold him on his way to the start my chance in the race was small.

I changed my plan of campaign. No longer would I ride a normal race, now I would have to drop back from the others, and kid him that he was not racing at all.

'Under starters orders,' the loud speaker boomed. Major Peter Thin mounted his rostrum, and called 'Come up at the back.' Not on your life, I thought for I wanted to be slowly away.

With a crash the starting tapes flew up and the field surged forward with myself just where I wanted to be, five lengths adrift. For the first thirty yards One Seven Seven switched off as planned, and was a perfect gentleman. As we moved over to the rails to take the first bend, he realised this was business after all. He took hold of his bit and with every stride gained on the field.

Although now out of control I thought that he would be satisfied when we caught up with the horse in front, but no, his blood was up, he was a racehorse and as each horse was passed his enthusiasm grew. Coming out of the long bend we rushed headlong at the first fence which took on massive proportions as each stride swept me nearer. When he saw the white wings of the fence beside him One Seven Seven lurched forwards and upwards, but alas not up enough. He crashed through the fence and was brought to his knees, catapulting me out of the saddle.

Jay Trump duly won at Sandown, thus my incident was not quite so important and no rocket was delivered, nevertheless I had to wait three months before I had the chance to redeem myself with my next ride. During that period I thought hard

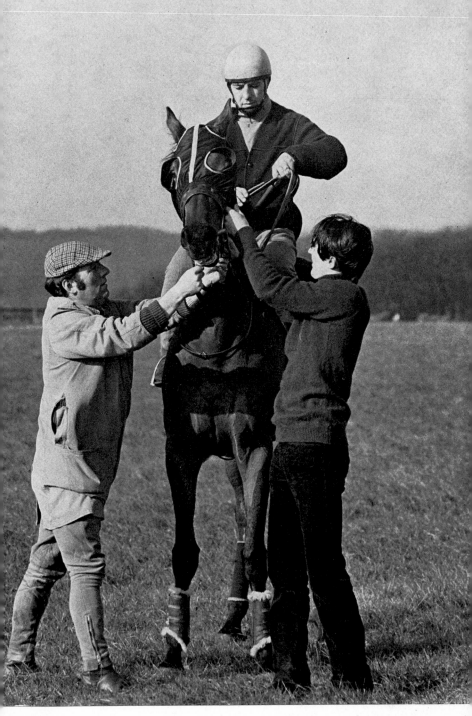

Putting the blinkers on before schooling. Brian Delaney on the left and the Right Hon. S. Stanhope (assistant trainer) on the right

Pendil in full flight at Kempton Park

'Come on, we can beat this lot with our eyes closed!' Pendil and me in
the Cheltenham Gold Cup

Grand National morning in the sauna bath, thank goodness for the bubbly

A turkish bath is much easier – and, as for the *Sporting Life*, it provides essential 'sporting' coverage

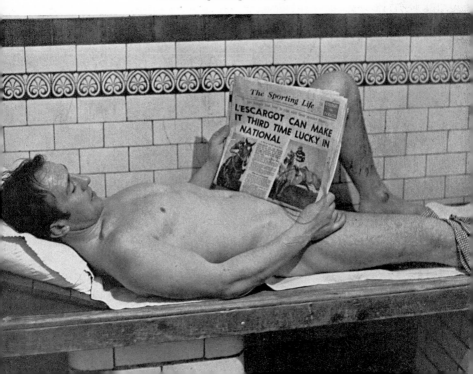

'It was tough out there', explaining to Ron Smyth why I did not win

'What do you think of this one Willie?'
'******* awful!'

Win or lose, the
Guv'nor was always the
same, a quick pat said
everything.

below: Defeated by a
short head in the
Cheltenham Gold Cup

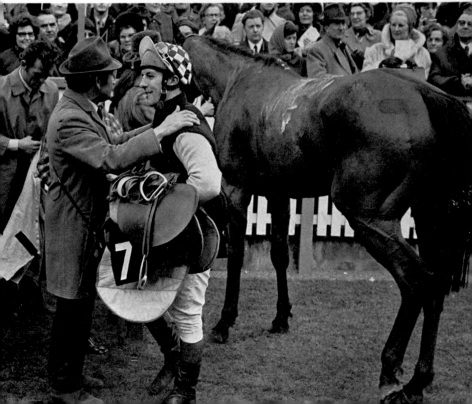

The ups and downs of a National Hunt jockey. Vickrom and I went on to win this race by 6 lengths

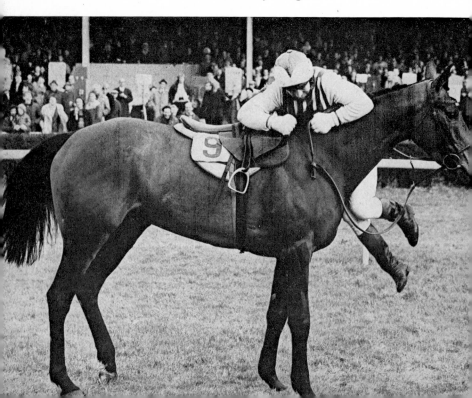

The 'other' half – Jennie Pitman

The whole family, Mark, Jennie, Paul and 'Titch'

My first gallop, note the Wellington boots – not an auspicious start

Rossagio – my first ever ride in public

about myself and only then did the truth come home. I was
not God's gift to racing after all—indeed, I was extremely
moderate. It had taken four years to sink in. I knew now that
it was going to be uphill all the way.

5 Learning at last

I could understand now that experience has to be earned. A week later One Seven Seven won as easily as he should have done with me. This time Willie Robinson rode him. '*Chase-form*' summed it up, 'Jumped well, always going well, took up the running approaching last, won easily.' I was now indeed humbled but had I won on him that first time, I would have been unbearable. My attitude changed, I realised my faults and tried hard to rectify them. The Guv'nor put me right. He sat me down in his office and spoke quietly of what was wanted.

'Richard, present your horse at his fences, well balanced and with a clear sight of the obstacle, ride to my orders and for God's sake practise your finish on the arm of the sofa.' He went on to say that I rode the worst finish he had ever seen, but if I was honest and gave him my loyalty I would ride many winners for him. He was true to his word with me. Now his present crop of jockeys possess these qualities, having reaped the rewards of the same advice.

It was several months before I rode in public for the Guv'nor again, a period of penance you might say. On 30 December 1964 I went to Fontwell Park to ride Indian Spice in a chase limited to inexperienced riders. The horse jumped extremely well, was always on the bridle and won hard held by twelve lengths.

An awful truth came home to me at this point. After years of trying to ride a winner and thinking it was the be all and end all I had now ridden one, but had done nothing clever to do so. The horse was by far the best in the race and would have won who ever had ridden it. Up to that point I had lived to ride. Now I realised that I would have to ride to live. The

Sporting Life the next day read 'Pitman Rides Winner At 60th Attempt'. It sounded as if I had won a consolation race at the local horse show. But at least I had finally started on the winning side, and only once more did I have to suffer the frustration of such a long losing run. That was in 1970, just as my best years were about to start. They were preceded by a remarkably bleak period when I rode 86 consecutive losers. To start with I just accepted that luck was against me and it would soon change. When it didn't I imagined all sorts of things. Was I riding badly? Should I have a rest, had I gone stale? And even, 'was my nerve going'? The body blow was delivered, not by anyone in racing circles, but by a petrol pump attendant on the M1 motorway. Returning from Nottingham, thoroughly dejected at yet another day without a winner, I pulled into the service area at Watford. After a meal and a strong coffee I felt much better and proceeded to fill up my petrol tank. The attendant greeted me with a cheerful, 'Hello Sir'. He studied me as he washed the dead flies from the windscreen and headlights. 'Do I know you?' he said uncertainly. Then with much more strength in his voice. 'Yes I do, you're the bloke who can't ride a winner, no how.' Fame at last! I was known for not riding winners. It transpired that a leading newspaper had been following jockeys with long losing runs and Pitman topped the charts.

When the tide turns the reverse applies. Horses win in spite of their rider, not because of him, and when things are going wrong nothing one does produces success. It was circumstances, or fate or what you will, that enabled me to record my next winners of that 1964–65 season.

After Indian Spice had obliged at Fontwell I had been riding more regularly. It was now a week away from the Easter holiday with its glut of race meetings. Fred Winter had decided to run three horses in one race at Chepstow, thus enabling Eddie Harty, Red Weaver and myself to ride. Eddie was riding Givenaway, the most fancied of the trio, Red was on Spaniards Close and I was on Sea Weed II, a nice little French horse. The day before the race all three did their final gallop together, putting the finishing touches to their training programme. Unfortunately Givenaway sustained an injury and was not declared to run the following day, thus leaving my mount as the favourite to win the race. Now Eddie, ever quick to see an opportunity, approached me that evening with a proposition. If he got me three rides at Towcester could he ride Sea Weed II at Chepstow? I did not like the idea much and decided to ask Fred Winter for advice. He said I ought to take three certain fees rather than one possible winner. Not completely convinced I asked him if he would still fancy Sea Weed II if I rode him. His reply made up my mind, 'The horse would probably win if either of you ride him, although much can go wrong before you reach the winning post.'

The horses at Towcester were now to be ridden by myself claiming a 7 lb. allowance for inexperience, and Sea Weed II, who was quoted at odds on, by Eddie Harty.

On arriving at the racecourse I found Bill Shand-Kydd who owned all three of my rides. He told me that one was coughing; now I was down to two and the deal did not look so good now. Savonarola won the seller easily under my guidance and the second, Minute Gun, also obliged us by keeping his head in front. My first great day; both mounts winners; champagne with the jubilant owner; a month's wages in my pocket; and prospects of more mounts. Sea Weed II? He finished 7th of 19 runners.

Bill Shand-Kydd, the international sportsman, had said to me after the second winner, 'If there is anything that I can do for you just ask, I can only say no, I can't bite you.' He was true to his word. A large white Rolls-Royce was sent to take my delighted and surprised bride to church for our wedding, an action which helped to change my outlook on life a little more. I realised that he had as much pleasure in giving as I had in receiving his generosity. Since that day I have never been too embarrassed to take gifts and have reciprocated whenever I could, with my time and services, small in comparison but all I have to give.

This series of circumstances not only enabled me to bring my meagre score to three winners for the 1964–65 season, it also gave me a regular supply of 'spare' rides. Various other trainers now started to follow suit, thus enabling me to double my score the following season.

At that time two incidents which have remained burned into my memory took place. I was given my first chance to win a big race, the Imperial Cup at Sandown Park. My mount was a novice hurdler running in a big really competitive handicap for the first time and as his rider I was also a novice riding in a big race for the first time. Wise elders of steeplechasing would never advise putting two novices together, but luckily for me Fred Winter did what he thought was right. Royal Sanction won the cup despite me, not because of me.

Of late I had been mis-hitting horses in a tight finish, that is, down their girth, so the Guv'nor had told me before the race that if I thought the horse needed a slap, look round to select the spot, give him one reminder then ride him out with hands and heels. The race went well for me, and after making steady progress I swept past Jeff King on First Audition to lead two hurdles from home. With victory in sight my horse began to idle, so the Guv'nor's advice, which I now realise was sarcasm, came into mind. In full view of the public I stood bolt upright, turned around in my stirrups, selected the correct spot and delivered the reminder.

Royal Sanction felt my body weight change rapidly several times and picked up his bridle. Thinking I had gone completely mad, he made for home. He passed the post with four lengths to spare, his jubilant jockey exhausted and oblivious of the spectacle he had provided! The punters who had backed me set up a cheer, but the professional racegoers felt sorry for this young jockey who had played polo between the last two flights. A little good comes out of every bad occasion. I was allowed to view the camera patrol and I realised beyond doubt that something would have to be done before I was very much older. Fred Winter has always forgiven mistakes so long as a jockey does not make the same one twice and although I never became an artist in a finish I certainly improved from that day on.

The second incident was costly as well as embarrassing for all concerned. I had ridden for Captain Ryan Price on three occasions that season, pleasing him on each. The fourth time was in a National Hunt Centenary Cup race at Fontwell Park. The horse, Burlington II, which had already won eight times that season, was owned by Major Derek Wigan, a steward of the meeting. The Jockey Club had given twenty cups to celebrate the National Hunt centenary, to be competed for all over the country. 'Cups' is misleading; they were of a size that Jack would have found at the top of the beanstalk, and none of us racing for it that day were likely to be present for the second centenary. Captain Price went to another race meeting so Major Wigan gave me my orders.

'Ride a sensible race, pick the opposition off one by one, and go on to lead after the last hurdle.' The Major went on to say that he really wanted this particular cup; the money was not important. I had ridden in the two previous races without success and sweating profusely I hurriedly grabbed my saddle which had been prepared by my valet. By-passing the trial scales I presented myself to be weighed by the Clerk of the Scales. He checked my number, my colours and finally to see if I carried the correct weight. Having satisfied himself all was well I was passed correct to ride and hurriedly gave the saddle, weight cloth and breastplate to Snowy, the 'Captain's' travelling head man, so that he could tack up Burlington II, whilst I made the last minute adjustments to my riding clothes.

During the race my mount was travelling so well I waited quite confidently until after the last hurdle before going to win. He won by four lengths in the short distance from the last flight of hurdles to the winning post—it could have been three times as much had I wished. From the moment that I pulled up to the time I rode victoriously into the winner's enclosure I had worked out my 10 per cent present and had already spent it in my mind. Everyone was overjoyed. Cheers and congratulations rang out all around the winner's enclosure

—until I sat on the scales to be weighed in. The official in charge looked hard into my eyes as if trying to find an explanation; for what I thought to myself? Then he spoke:

'Pitman, is that some sort of a joke?'

'What sir?' I replied.

'Good God, man, you are a stone light.'

Very slowly, I realised he was deadly serious. I looked at the scales and then at my equipment. Bewildered, I dragged myself into the changing room to hear the loudspeaker booming the news that Number 5, Burlington II had been disqualified for the rider failing to draw the correct weight.

The inevitable enquiry was held. I was acquitted of any blame, the Clerk of the Scales carrying the can for weighing me out incorrectly. This, of course, was no consolation to Major and Mrs Wigan who minutes earlier had arms outstretched to collect the prized Centenary Cup. Ryan Price said to Josh Gifford that evening 'It's a good job we are not short of winners.' It was a severe blow, because Captain Price never asked me to ride for his stable again.

But when one door shuts another usually opens. My services were now being used regularly by Major Verly Bewicke. Although we did not achieve a winner I managed to get horses to complete that had not done so of late. He would, I am sure, be the first to admit that his charges at that time were below par; but then that was also true of myself.

My last ride for the Major that season was In Haste in the Scottish National at Ayr. I was tailed off after being prominent for two miles and trailed in a long time after the winner. I experienced the most peculiar sensation when driving my horse along over the third mile. My body seized up completely; only my brain and my eyes continued to work. There I was in the crouching position, not able to do a thing to stop my tired steed from jumping the remaining fences. Being a sensible horse he popped each obstacle as it came, only to pull up after the winning post and follow the stragglers into the paddocks. Movement started to come back now, and after clumsily dismounting I tried to explain what had happened; but to my dismay I could only hear my words inside my head, not through the ear. The Major motioned me to the weighing room before I became too much of an embarrassment to all concerned. It transpired that I had wasted too hard in an attempt to do the correct weight of 9 st. 7lb. In doing so I had removed a greater amount of salt from the body than was healthy, thus a form of cramp set in. That was the start of my weight troubles.

How severe they were can be judged from the fact that now, in my retirement, my riding weight is around 11 st. 7lb.—and I am in good health and not overweight. I was at last learning what was required to make a jockey besides riding ability.

6 My first, first jockey's job

I married Jenny, the girl I had met in Cheltenham where she then 'did her two' for Major Champneys, on 2 October 1965 in Leicester, where her father George Harvey farmed. My best man was Brian Delaney and for moral support we took Derek King along. On our way from Lambourn to Leicester we passed through Coventry, or rather we did a tour of the town eventually coming out on the Lambourn road. Brian was convinced that this was a bad omen: we ought to carry on back to Lambourn for the marriage would never last.

However we continued our journey. The blazing lights of a steak house attracted us in, whereupon I was violently sick in the car park. That really convinced Brian that marriage was not for me, and it was only under extreme pressure that he was persuaded to continue the journey. We three were billeted with some friends, Florrie and Walter Dodd, and they looked after us really well. I was told the next morning the extra money that I had found in my jacket had been won at cards during a period when the demon drink had taken over my mind.

As I was being driven up the long avenue leading to the church door, I spotted the white Rolls-Royce that was conveying Jenny about to reach the steps. My driver put his foot down hard, screeched to a halt in front of the Rolls, bundled Brian and me out in a heap and beat a hasty retreat! The wedding over and the reception a success, it was time to be alone at last. My bride was in tears because I had forgotten to tell her that I had agreed to give a pal a lift to our honeymoon spot 150 miles away.

Not the most auspicious start to a marriage and more was

to come. I had contracted yellow jaundice, so every day of our honeymoon poor Jenny was jumping and kicking while I spent my time with my head in the sink. Despite all this, and Brian's foreboding, ten years later our marriage is still intact —although a clash of temperaments has been known from time to time!

Three months later Jenny was not feeling well, so on my way to work I called in to see Major Champneys who was employing her. 'Afraid Jenny won't be in today Major, I think she has caught my yellow jaundice.' His reply stopped me in my tracks. 'She will wish it was jaundice Pip. It takes nine months to recover from what she's got.' He was right of course: Jenny produced our first son eleven months after we married, and now I really needed to ride for a living. I was present at the birth and the first glimpse of my son and that first cry was the most marvellous thing I have ever witnessed. It was music to my ears then, of course; over the next five years the charm wore off. I remember telling Jenny that I would never subject her to it again; alas five months later she was on the way again!

We looked for a house, but with little success at first, mainly through lack of funds and, because of the way I had been riding, the lack of prospects. Fulke Walwyn let us have a cottage until something could be found, which was a year later. I was lucky enough to meet a sympathetic building society manager. Having patiently listened to my plight he agreed to forward me enough money to purchase a new semi-detached bungalow near Lambourn. Luckily I was able to re-pay my debt quite quickly, for Lady Luck started to smile upon me.

For it was at this time—1966—Major Verly Bewicke asked me if I would like to ride for his stable as first jockey: he would pay me a retainer and I could live in one of his houses. I was naturally both delighted and surprised because at that time I had ridden only ten winners, a meagre total for six years work, and was still claiming 7 lb. After talking it over with Fred Winter (he said I ought to jump at the chance) and with Jenny, who agreed but with reservations, the bargain was struck. I did not move to the Major's cottage for two reasons. Firstly my bungalow was my castle, and secondly I thought that I would commit myself too closely if I moved to a tied cottage. I must say that the start of the 1966–67 season, my first as a first jockey, felt good. I was contracted to ride for the Major and make myself available to school his horses on two mornings a week. This was indeed satisfactory, because it enabled me to stay with Fred Winter in the same capacity as before.

The season started well for me with three rides on the first day and one winner, for Ivor Herbert. It seemed that I was moving at last? I have never stopped learning to this day and an important lesson was noted on the second day of the meeting: Never shut the door completely. Bill Marshall asked me to ride Mr Polpeck in a lads' race. He was confident that it would win! In the paddock I was greeted with a customary, 'Hello, Matey,' and given precise instructions as to how I would win the race. As I was leaving the paddock, almost as an afterthought, he said, 'I've tightened the girths. They won't need touching.' At the start force of habit made me put my hand under the saddle flap to check my girths. They were quite loose. I instinctively asked the starter's assistant to tighten them. It should be remembered that they are professional men. I duly rode my race strictly to orders, getting up on the line to win by a head. To my dismay as we walked back to the winner's enclosure the public address informed everyone that Number 5 Mr Polpeck was second.

I was stunned! It appeared that a lot of the punters were upset as well because they formed a circle around the judges box shouting all kinds of abuse and holding him a prisoner. Bill was blind to all this as he strode up to where I was unsaddling my sweating partner.

'What the—hell were you doing, getting those—girths tightened?' He obviously had been watching the start through his binoculars. I tried to explain that the horse had 'blown out' during his canter to the post, loosening the girths.

'Are you—well trying to tell me that I don't know my—job?' I lost my temper and exchanged adjective for adjective before reaching the safety of the weighing room.

I was never asked to ride for Bill Marshall again, but the lesson was learned. I had shut the door behind me. If I had said I was sorry and that I had forgotten his last order, I might have ridden some of the many winners he has turned out since. So after two days of the new season I had been walking on air and then brought to earth with a bang.

My new job took me to places that had been names before, Ayr, Hexham, and the most northern of courses, Perth. The last is probably the most sporting of all racetracks in the British Isles. Punters there bet for enjoyment only, cheering the horses three fences from the post. It is not only the winner who is greeted on his return to the enclosure, but all three placed horses receive recognition for their efforts. The racecourse itself is very picturesque, set behind Scoone Palace and bordered by an active salmon river. The directors of the racecourse are all keen sportsmen themselves, and in dry times they bring the water carts from their farms to fetch and distribute the river water over the baked turf.

A sad aspect of the job is that so many familiar faces disappear from the weighing room every year through continuous injury or plain bad luck. It was at Perth races that I first met one such chap although our paths were to cross many times during the next two years. Racing folks knew him as 'Bones' Nightingale, I suppose because he was 5 ft. 10 in. high and only 8 st. 7 lb. in weight. 'Bones' believed that trainers would not give rides to lads with big feet because time had taught them that boys would grow to match their feet, becoming too heavy to make jockeys. The answer for 'Bones' was to cram his size $9\frac{1}{2}$ feet into size 7 jodhpur boots every morning. This ruse worked and he duly got his rides, but being so devoid of natural cushioning he broke something nearly every time he fell, and eventually without any notice disappeared from the riding scene.

Characters like him make the changing room what it is. The

wages are poor for all but the top twelve jump jockeys. For the less fortunate lads a time comes when the hope that has kept them going through long periods of bad luck and injury finally fades. But for each face that is missing the start of the season brings two fresh ones, each convinced that he is to be the next Josh Gifford or Terry Biddlecombe.

My first season as a first jockey was, although not very successful, full of new experiences. I rode the light weights for Miss Auriol Sinclair, a professional trainer of the highest degree. She provided me with several winners and also a chance to race against Arkle. Sunny Bright was the horse I rode, a novice who in his trainer's eyes would be second to Arkle, but not disgraced. Everything about that great horse was as I had been told. His entrance to the paddock at Ascot was not unlike a great ballet dancer, who pauses on entering the stage, just long enough to approve of the eager audience, and then parades with an air of majesty. His canter to the starting gate was that of an athlete, and he strung out the field before halfway with contemptuous ease.

My orders were to settle Sunny Bright down over the first three fences, establishing a relaxed rhythm, and gradually to increase my pace from Swinley Bottom quickening up the straight. The settling part was easy, for Arkle made the pace so quick that no other horse was pulling hard. Sure enough as we turned out of Swinley Bottom Sunny Bright quickened in response to my urging. We gained ground fence by fence until, as we turned for home, I was within striking distance of Arkle. Without looking round Pat Taffe accelerated away brushing aside my challenge, no more than an irritation, as if it never really existed. We finished second by some twelve lengths. Miss Sinclair had not been far wrong with the assessment of her novice chaser.

A strange thing happened in the Halloween Chase at Newbury later that season, starting with a dreadful sinking feeling as something went wrong followed by the split second decision needed to right the situation. I was riding Woodbow, a really promising novice chaser, owned by Norman Gardner. He was a superb owner who had endured the worst luck imaginable with every horse that he had had with Fred Winter. At last we thought his patience was being rewarded, for Woodbow had won his only two novice chases and was now bowling along twenty lengths clear of his field with seven fences to jump. His jumping had been an exhibition and had carried him clear of his field, the only thing I had to do now was to steer him to the post.

At that moment there was a sharp crack; my stirrup had snapped clean in half and suddenly I was falling down one side. Without thinking I immediately leant down, grabbed and opened the stirrup leather at the same time, and kicked home my boot. But I was now riding with one knee seven inches higher that the other, six inches above the horse's wither. The result was a shifting of my body weight which tilted me to such a degree that I was in danger of falling off the opposite side, as we hurtled towards the next fence. I caught hold of the neck strap and thus stayed aboard until the finish was reached safely, if somewhat haphazardly. Peter Bromley commentating for the BBC said to his listeners 'Woodbow is running all over the course as if he is drunk.'

The connections were, of course, very pleased when they saw the evidence although most other people thought that I should have kicked out my other stirrup as Tim Brookshaw did once in the Grand National. Bryan Marshall was the only person who said I had done right, because my mount was at that time still running very free and standing off his fences from just inside the wings. He went on to explain that had I kicked out my other iron the force of Woodbow's jump would sooner or later have catapulted me from the saddle. Many times during the next eight years I had to do things instinctively, and I was usually successful.

I was now riding with welcome regularity on better horses at the big tracks. But race riding runs very hot and cold, and as I learnt again towards the end of the season it is a great leveller. Minute Gun was a novice chaser with the Totalisator Novice Champion Chase at the Cheltenham March meeting as his objective. He was not a natural jumper of fences, so I nursed him over the first two miles before I really started to put him into the race. With every stride I gained ground on the leaders. My blood was really up and I was thinking of victory on my home track. I asked for a 'big one' at the downhill fence. Had I negotiated it cleanly the race would have been within my grasp.

But Minute Gun, alas, was not used to being bustled. He panicked and snatched at the fence and paid the penalty. When we both stopped rolling down the muddy slope I remembered Fred Winter's words: 'You can't win if you don't get round.' Sitting there wet and miserable I could see in the distance horses and riders fighting out the finish that I had thought would concern me.

Despite this set-back, Bill Shand-Kydd, Minute Gun's owner, asked me if I would like to ride in the Grand National the next month because he had broken his arm and did not think that he would be fit enough to ride himself. This was a great moment for me. A rider's first National is surrounded by mystery and intrigue. The blood-curdling tales of former jockey's combined with the hard luck stories or triumphs only added to my burning desire to win that great race. Sadly, I never did.

My partner that year was to be a proven handicapper called Dorimont. He had very useful form in Ireland before Bill bought him with this race in mind. The preliminaries were all that I expected them to be, except that I was virtually ignored by the photographers who clammered around the leading lights with fancied rides. That was a small blow to my pride, but it was forgotten the moment the race started. Then it was every man to himself. As the field raced to the first I had a good position just behind the leaders. After having galloped across the cinders on the Melling road I realised why so many jockeys wore goggles even though the ground was not heavy. I was so heavily showered with dust that I could not see the first fence, though I suppose that this was probably an advantage. Dorimont jumped it with ease. It seems easy enough, I thought to myself as the second thorn fence loomed up. Again we sailed over without touching a twig.

On the outside several horses fell, causing two more to be brought down with shouts and thuds. I had no time to think of them because the third was looming up. I had forgotten that it was an open ditch though it was only a few hours before that I had walked the course to plan my race. I remembered too late: it was a five-foot three-inch fence with a six-foot ditch.

'Kick like hell,' I heard someone shout, so I did. Dorimont stood off a stride, too soon, launched himself into the air and to my horror started his descent before the fence had been reached. The noise was deafening as we crashed to the ground, and it increased as the field galloped over me as I lay crouched. As the noise died away a friendly voice gave me the all clear. I was not hurt physically, but my pride was severely dented. I remember leaning on the rails wishing that the race could be restarted just so that I could have a second chance to prove myself.

I had not covered myself with glory at Aintree, nor indeed through the whole of the 1966–67 season, but I had at last experienced many important new facets of the racing scene. I now felt that I would be one day genuinely worthy of the title 'first jockey.'

7 *Schooling*

A young jockey stayed with me for a few days at the end of that season. As it was a slack time I didn't ride out at morning exercise in order to look after him before going racing each day. On returning to the trainer he said that he no longer wished to 'do his two' because Richard Pitman did not have to work. How wrong he was! That same jockey has been drifting ever since because he won't take his jacket off to buckle down to work. Hundreds of lads ride really well but only the ones who deserve rides through hard work, cleanliness and loyalty reap the rewards.

My usual day at that time would go as follows. After I had schooled at Major Bewicke's first thing in the morning I would then dash twenty-five miles to Aldbourne to school for Mrs Lomax during breakfast time, thus enabling me to get to Lambourn in time for Fred Winter's second lot. The morning's work finished I would then drive to the races, ride four or five horses and finally drive home. My day was not finished even then, for there would be at least ten phone calls to make and the next day's form to study. One thing is certain: what you lack in ability you must make up for with effort!

Schooling in general can be an enjoyable exercise, or, more often, a 'hairy' morning where tempers run high. A lot depends on the trainer's nature, the number of horses involved and, of course, having the right jockey to school with. The important thing is to concentrate on doing the job in hand, not trying to show up your fellow schooling jockey. Eddie Harty was not the easiest partner to school with, whilst Bobby Beasley was a joy to watch; but the jockey who taught me the most about schooling was without a doubt Paul Kellaway, a true professional in every sense. Paul explained carefully after our first school together that there was no prize for the first one to reach the end of the schooling ground.

'It's easier to get a horse buzzing than to settle one down,' he said. 'So just relax, let your horse know *how* he got to the other side of the fence, we can always quicken him a bit when he's done that properly. A rapport developed between Paul and myself, extending to Vic Soane and Johnny Francome, who in turn passed it on to the younger lads. So the schooling at Fred Winter's is less 'hairy' than most.

I remember one particularly cold morning when Johnny had gone to ride for a permit holder first thing. There was no sign of him twenty minutes after the appointed time to school, so tight-lipped, and with eyes like slits, the Guv'nor barked the orders to start. It was an unpleasant situation. We were cold, late and hurriedly re-arranged, all waiting for the first mistake and the explosion which, under these circumstances, would follow. However just as we were showing the horses what they had to jump, Johnny appeared on foot from the opposite direction, red-faced and out of breath. 'Sorry Guv'nor,' he panted, 'I thought that you meant the little hurdles down in the valley and now my car's stuck.' Instead of exploding, Fred Winter replied quietly, but with an unmistakable air of sarcasm, 'I'm sorry John, it's all my fault. I ought to get a bloody great blackboard twenty foot square and write the orders in white paint.' The message was quite clear and neither John nor any of those present was ever late again.

I will try to explain how a schooling morning is conducted at Fred Winter's, although methods differ from stable to stable. First the schooling ground, which is located next to the gallops, consists of six sets of fences of varying heights, each set having two plain fences and one open ditch. There are also three sets of hurdles ranging from eighteen inches high to three foot six inches which is racecourse size. So there are twenty-seven jumps in this communal schooling area which supplies twelve different trainers with the necessary facilities.

Things can be edgy when several trainers want to school at the same time.

Fred Winter trains a string of fifty-five horses. The older horses need an occasional refresher course, while the novices require much more attention. The importance of schooling young horses cannot be over-emphasized: jumping is the name of the game. The horses taking part in the Wednesday session are listed in pairs or threes with their respective jockeys and leave the yard in the same order at six minute intervals enabling the first batch to finish just before the next arrives at the schooling ground. This way horses do not fret or hot up before they start, it is important to be in a relaxed state of mind in order to perform to the best of their ability.

This particular day sees Osbaldeston, a fiery little individual, going on his own because he is so keen in company that it makes him oblivious to his rider's instructions. As it is he gallops much faster than is normally safe, his speed giving him the impetus he needs to take off at his jumps two strides before he should do. The Guv'nor and I, standing by the second fence will watch John and Ossey fly the obstacle, both thinking it far safer to be where we are rather than on his back. On returning, John says that he thinks that once is enough and the Guv'nor, with a twinkle in his eye, agrees. As Ossey's protective boots are removed and his legs checked for cuts, the second contingent arrives. This time there are three horses Crisp, What Next and Noble Neptune, two experienced jumpers and one novice chaser. We mount our horses only to find the stirrup leathers are too long or too short. They must be altered before we start because, if the jockey is not comfortable he will not ride to his best, thus a school may be wasted and time is important with so many horses to get through.

Crisp is a seasoned campaigner. He feels me relax my grip when I fumble for the stirrup leather, and as he plunges forward the Guv'nor has to jump to safety, shouting, 'You silly old sod!' (I presume he means the horse!) Having anchored him I return to get my orders.

'Richard, lead the other two over the small fences. If the novice jumps well take them over the middle fences straight away.' Old Crisp knows what is required of him and before I give him the signal, has whipped round to face the fences, the other two following some twenty-five yards behind. My fellow skips over the three fences in faultless fashion. Behind me I hear a noise as some birch is kicked out by the novice and the voice of the master saying. 'Give him his head, go with him.' We decide that the bigger fences will suit him better—'Give him more to think about' says Vic Soane. He is dead right. The horse, What Next, doesn't touch a twig this time. As we trot back to the Guv'nor with smiles all over our faces, I think to myself how marvellous this life is, to get paid for something that I enjoy so much.

The grins are soon wiped off because the next lot are three excited and sweaty colts, newly arrived from Newmarket. From past experiences we know that they will have hard mouths and a distinct dislike of hurdles. A fourth, older horse, ridden by a young hopeful, is there to lead us in indian file over the baby hurdles. This is a dual purpose school; we are to teach the new horses to jump and the experienced hurdler is to lead us at the same time giving a hopeful young jockey chance to prove himself. All goes well the first time. They appear to like it after all and have even stopped sweating, but second time up two of them are not so sure, they peep about looking for an easy way out, so firm handling is necessary. If they get away with it they will try it on even more next time: sure enough the third school is good.

When the boots are taken off the Guv'nor pats them, at the same time giving each a handful of grass to eat and telling them what good chaps they are. This is to make them associate jumping with a pleasant time so that they will not resent the next lesson. This is essential: every school finished on a good note. Should a horse not jump well he will go again, within reason, until he does jump well.

The fourth and last school of this particular session is made up of four experienced hurdlers which are due to race the following day. Usually the runners would have a sprint to clear their windpipes, but to relieve the monotony of continual galloping the Guv'nor decides to let them school instead, killing two birds with one stone: they get their final work done, and at the same time they are cheered up. I say cheered up, because that is just what happens when experienced horses school at home. Often a lazy galloper will get on his toes the moment the schooling boots and bandages are put on: He will pull hard as he skips over the obstacles. Heading home he will jig-jog, occasionally giving a nuck and a squeal showing his enjoyment of life in general.

This is one of Fred Winter's main training policies, to keep his horses in the right frame of mind throughout the ten months season. As the Guv'nor, Brian Delaney, John and myself drive slowly back to the stables the conversation is solely the happenings of that morning.

'That Ossey seems to have no brains until he meets a fence, then he knows just what to do,' says John, and Brian Delaney will chip in, 'When I was riding I would have given him rein, kicked him on and loved it.' I say that it makes you wonder why all horses don't jump as well as Crisp, it seems so effortless. 'Christ! he wants jam on it,' retorts the Guv'nor. We then discuss the merits of the young horses and what chance the runners have the following day. As we pull up in front of the office, Lawrence Elliot, the secretary, comes slowly to meet us to say that two owners had rung, the ground was heavy at Wincanton for the next day and would I ring Peter Cundell straight away.

Schooling mornings do not always go as smoothly as the one described, although falls are certainly rare. I can only recall falling on four occasions at home in the fifteen years I rode. The reason for this is that a horse is never allowed to get tired at home. He is always well-balanced and meets properly-sited fences on level ground. The schooling ground is to teach a horse the correct way to clear an obstacle without taking chances, whereas on the racecourse it is often a case of all or nothing, and two out of ten times you end up with nothing.

Another factor is that at home you are accompanied by an experienced horse acting as nanny, but the racecourse throws together perhaps twenty novices each knowing as little as the next.

The first time Fred Winter asked me to take a bad hurdles jumper over the fences I thought that he was joking, but he was not; and in fact the horse jumped fences really well, knowing that if he treated them with the contempt that he had for hurdles, the penalty would have to be paid. We immediately put the horse back over hurdles which he jumped correctly. After that we tried many horses over fences, solely because their hurdling was sloppy. The result was always remarkable. The best horse to have this treatment was Lanzarote. His jumping was either brilliant when on a good stride or diabolical if meeting a hurdle wrongly. He schooled twice over fences before the 1973 Champion Hurdle, jumping with precision and a deal of brain.

Very occasionally the Guv'nor decided that a horse would hurt someone long before he learned the finer points of jumping and so the owner was informed and asked to remove his steed. The importance of proper schooling cannot be stressed enough. To repeat Fred Winter, 'He can't win if he doesn't get round.'

8 Riding is only part of the job

A steeplechase jockey has many other jobs besides actually riding. Quite often that is almost the easiest part of it. To be really successful he must be a dietician, an acrobat and a showman, and drive long journeys. Although many jockeys share car journeys I was quite independent, particularly when Johnny came on the scene to relieve me of my duties as chauffeur to Fred Winter. The Guv'nor came to hate driving after his long riding career so when he started training the job of driving him to the races fell to his jockeys.

I remember the first time I drove his Mercedes Benz. It was to Plumpton, a journey of some two and a half hours along very twisty lanes. He made up for the wasted time by doing his entries for some weeks ahead, occasionally looking at me over the top of his glasses to ask my advice about a course suiting a horse. When this was completed he would carefully pack everything away, take off his glasses and settle down to sleep. This was the opportunity for me to enjoy myself. My foot went hard down and I would test the Mercedes' cornering ability and acceleration until I was forced to brake sharply. I then cast a glance towards my sleeping boss, only to see that his right eye was glaring at me.

'Didn't you have any toys when you were a boy, Richard?' I took his point—and reverted to sensible driving.

My busiest season was 1972–73 during which I drove 66,000 miles in my own car, as well as journeys in other people's. Jockeys are charged very high premiums by insurance companies, yet they are mostly better than average drivers. Riding and driving have many things in common: one must be able to make split-second decisions, anticipate other people's actions and have a well-developed sense of speed. I have never been involved in an accident during the fifteen years that I have driven to the races, although two tyres have burst at speed and nine windscreens have been shattered. All but one of these windscreens were broken by stones. The other one was struck by a golf ball: it had been mishit by a police-man practising his tee shots after a hard day catching speeding motorists. It was a fine irony that one of his victims that morning had been myself as I journeyed to Warwick races, late as usual.

The impact, noise and sudden loss of vision were startling, but then I was used to violent changes of situation. I stopped and, having picked the golf ball from my lap, I got out to take stock of the situation. The road was deserted except for one man who was strolling towards me, whistling nonchalantly with both hands behind his back. When he came abreast of my car I could see that it was the policeman who had 'pinched' me that same morning. Now with reddened cheeks he was half concealing a golf club behind his back. This time his voice was embarrassed rather than harsh, and I had to smile at the reversal of the situations.

I only once missed a booked ride because of car trouble. The journey to Plumpton had always taken me two and a half hours, without stopping for petrol or to quench my thirst, but on this particular day I had the first of my two burst tyres. A quick change took me ten minutes, but then I found a slow puncture in my spare tyre the moment I released the jack. After a walk to the nearest garage and a bribe to the attendant I finally set off again an hour after my enforced stop.

A jockey ought to be present at least three-quarters of an hour before his first ride. The latest he may present himself to the Clerk of the Scales being fifteen minutes before the scheduled start, failing which a substitute rider is weighed out for a ride. On reflection, the headlong dash to make up the lost time was scarcely worth the £15 riding fee I would receive at the end of the day. Arriving on the course twenty minutes before the off, I forced my way into the members' car park and left my car, with the engine running, to the irate attendant whilst I vaulted the rails on to the track. To my dismay as I breathlessly burst into the weighing room I saw Paul Kellaway handing over his saddle to my trainer: I was too late.

The stipendary steward informed me that the stewards would want to see me after the second race in their room directly above the jockeys' changing quarters. Access to this room is by an ancient spiral staircase and as I climbed it the barracking from the boys was unmerciful.

'They've been after you for some time Dick'; 'It'll be a £20 fine at least'; 'Talk your way out of this one Pitman!' The room was small, housing a table, four chairs and a projector for the showing of patrol films. Three stewards were seated behind the table and to their right a very pretty woman was sitting holding a pad and pencil. Our small enquiry was simple enough, but the language a hot-blooded farmer uses when he feels he has been robbed of a race, meant that she had to write words that never cropped up on her secretarial course.

My explanation was accepted by a majority decision. I was to be cautioned this time and warned to leave enough time in future for breakdowns. My descent into the centre of the changing room was not unlike being lowered into a goldfish bowl. All eyes were upon me eagerly awaiting the verdict. When I reached the foot of the stairs I slapped my left hand with my right saying, 'Naughty boy Pitman don't do it again.' An ominous silence was broken by a voice from behind: 'I think you had better come back upstairs Pitman'—the leading steward had followed me down the spiral staircase, only to hear my 'contempt of court'. As a result I was fined £10. The day was a remarkable financial failure. I had earned nothing, and my expense consisted of petrol £8, puncture and bribe £2 and £10 fine: A day's trading had cost me £20, five hours at the wheel and probably a lost connection.

The only light relief from travelling came when I was asked to ride at the racetracks of Wye and Folkestone. My workmates and I would travel to London by train, change at Waterloo and head through the hop fields and orchards of Kent, playing cards as we went. These journeys without fail produced new acquaintances from every walk of life and every part of London, real characters all of them, even the rogues being likeable. To sit amongst them listening to accounts of championship fights they *knew* had been thrown, of greyhounds that were certainties and of football players who were past it was indeed a welcome break. On the return journeys the conversation was totally racing.

'That was a great race Mellor rode in the novice chase,' said a man who had obviously backed him. 'Yes, but he only had Biddlecombe to beat, Stan's worth two lengths from the last fence' replies his friend. A weather-beaten man who had obviously seen better days chipped in, 'You lot don't know a good jockey when you see one, I remember...' and was shouted down because they had all heard his well-worn stories before.

It was on such a trip that I met a fellow of my age who has remained a friend to this day. Bobby Colthorpe had been a physical training instructor in the army and now was clerk to several bookies, attracted by his love for the open air and racing itself. Bobby Colthorpe would talk highly intelligently and for hours about racing, never talking through his pockets as do many betting people. He had a friend in the fish trade and usually bore gifts of fresh mackerel, a dressed crab or whatever the boys requested (Johnny Haine was partial to Dover Sole), Bobby did this for the lads out of the goodness of his heart, not to get information as many people would think. Eventually he was saddled with the nickname 'Bobby the Fish.'

After unsuccessfully riding in six races at Kempton a tired sweating Pitman decided that a nice cold shower would put back what the day had taken out. Several unanswered pleas as to how long the occupant would be made me think that the shower had been left running by the previous user. I pulled the curtain back and was startled to see five dozen gleaming mackerel staring back at me. It transpired that they had been caught that morning for several jockeys to eat the same evening and needed to be kept as fresh as possible!

It was around this time that my weight began to worry me more and more. Although the travelling would constitute a job in itself, a well paid job at that, the wasting (losing weight) drained my energy resources. My weight started to rise quite slowly, gathering momentum as the years slipped by until it became a continual battle to ride at even 11 st. 3 lb. As a lad, full of youthful exuberance, I would run for miles in a sweatsuit in order to lose the vital 3 lb. overweight, returning to swathe in blankets in front of the fire to continue the process. An easier way is to go to sauna or Turkish baths which have become plentiful over the last decade. I found that the Turkish bath suited me far better than the Sauna, mainly because I do not like being enclosed for too long.

The sauna is basically an air-tight wooden box with slatted benches at varying heights to sit upon. Stones are heated by a well-designed heater until they almost glow, at which stage the occupant pours a ladle full of water on to them, resulting in a cloud of steam surging up and around the wooden cell. When using a sauna it is advisable to take an interesting book with you as boredom rather than discomfort tends to end a session prematurely: besides the furniture that I have des-cribed, there is just a thermometer and a very small window set into the door, all of which do not exactly occupy the mind for very long. A normal person could lose 5 lb. during one one and a half hour sitting.

The Turkish bath has much more to offer, besides losing weight. You can relax on a vibrating bed or have a massage.

On entering a Turkish bath for the first time I was shown around the various rooms and told of the uses of each before being allocated a cubicle consisting of a bed, locker and bedside table. After stripping off my clothes I ventured out armed only with a very small hand towel which I draped over one shoulder. I was, of course, the odd man out. Everybody else draped their towel over their lower regions whilst sitting in the rooms of their choice or walking about the baths. Although the Almighty when handing out manly qualities overlooked yours truly, several years frequenting jockeys changing rooms had removed any trace of embarrassment from me. The first room I entered was just comfortably hot, the second a sweating heat and the third damned uncomfortable.

The middle room was the most popular of all, with nearly all the deckchairs occupied by tired, overweight businessmen. I was young and strong and there would be no compromise for me: it was the hot room or nothing. Reading was difficult, due to the amount of sweat dripping from my forehead into my eyes and from my hands on the now tatty pages. Throwing the sodden mess to the floor I turned my attention to the tiled walls, discoloured by years of persistent heat. After forty-five minutes of counting each tile, its cracks and chips I felt my head spinning. I thought it would pass. It did not.

A sea of faces peering down at me and a hollow far-away voice were the next things I remember. The voice was telling someone to get a very sugary cup of tea for the jockey who had passed out in the hot room. John the masseur cleared everybody from the cubicle they had carried me to and told me to sleep. My dreams turned to nightmares of fire and of races snatched from my grasp. I tossed and turned whilst my troubled mind settled to fit in with the peace and quiet of my cool cubicle. I went home deeply worried. Was I weak? Would I be up to the falls and strains of a jump jockey's life if I could not stand heat? I had lost 4 lb., but the cost had been high.

Determined to find out my capabilities in this field I returned to the baths the next day, but this time I asked John to put me wise. He recommended a routine for me that I could repeat as many times as I wished without harm. Firstly a visit to the warm room. Just five minutes to help the body acclimatize and then into the steam room to open the pores. Then to the middle room. As I walked through the door I could see the entrance to the hot room, at which point I remembered what I had done the previous day, nature took command of my senses and I proceeded to retch from the pit of my stomach.

The answer was to sit with my back to that dreaded room, denying its very existence. After sweating well for an hour John advised me to take a plunge into the cold pool which seemed to electrify my whole body. For thirty seconds only I languished in the cold pool before starting the whole process again. I repeated the cycle four times before John called me to his marble slab for a massage and a good scrubbing down with a stiff brush. His expert hands, applying oil to my body, working away at tense muscles and displaced sinews left me feeling ten years younger than when I walked in. This session left me 6 lb. lighter after four and a half hours sweating. It was both encouraging and relaxing to do it in that fashion, but most times I had only two hours to lose the same weight. On those occasions it was a continual struggle against time and Mother Nature.

It was soul-destroying to check your weight every half hour only to find it was not coming down at the required rate and knowing full well the time to leave for the racetrack was closing. In these instances I would don a rubber sweat suit underneath a track suit, run to the car and drive to the race-course with the heater full on in order to lose those vital few pounds. There were, of course, enjoyable times to be had in the baths. Having taken a severe kicking by 30 galloping horses, but without breaking any bones, a jockey gets no sympathy, but none the less hurts like hell. The remedy I prescribed for myself in those cases was to call at the first off licence, buy a bottle of champagne and stop off at the nearest Turkish baths. The cold pool keeps the champagne at the correct temperature whilst my bruises are eased away by the masseur. A shower, a few glasses of bubbly in the warm room, and a new man emerges ready to tackle the unknown hazards the next day's racing will present.

9 *The falls*

There is no such thing as a nice fall. Even if you are not hurt you are not going to win the race lying on the turf with your feet in the air. Most jockeys will find that they fail to negotiate a race once in ten rides. This means a top jockey who will have 450 rides a season will fall around forty-five times, of which maybe five will hurt him enough to put him out of action from a few days to many months. The bulk of the falls just leave aching limbs and large areas of bruising. Worse is concussion, in spite of the ultra-modern crash helmets that are now obligatory. Forty-eight hours sleep will put this right in most cases. Then there are the irritating dislocations of shoulders, ankles, wrists and collar bones.

I say irritating because they are enough to stop you riding for a while, but not so serious as to enable you to make firm plans. Lastly, the injuries that we all fear are broken thighs, arms and shoulders and worst of all a fractured skull. These either put a jockey out of action for many months or finish his career altogether.

A medical record book was introduced by the Jockey Club in 1973 to protect jockeys from themselves, as many riders persistently rode before they were fit to do so. Although most got away with it, several jockeys did lasting damage to themselves, resulting in premature retirement and an unnecessary drain on the injury fund. The medical record book contains details of previous injuries and diseases on the first page and a list of injections received on the second. Two pages are left for recordable falls. Whenever a rider falls he must report to the Clerk of Scales and be examined by the doctor before he is passed fit to ride again. Should the doctor think the jockey unfit to continue riding that day he will record the fact with red ink in the rider's medical record book. Before being allowed to ride again a racecourse doctor must examine and pass fit the injured jockey, stating in writing that he is fit to ride.

Each entry is endorsed by the doctor's signature. Every day that a jockey rides he must show his book to the Clerk of Scales who will allow or disallow the rider from taking part in the day's proceedings, according to the colour of the last entry. A rider who fails to produce his book for clearance must undergo a rigorous examination by the course doctor and having been passed fit is fined £2 to improve his memory. It had been found that friendly GPs would pass a jockey fit if the jockey insisted he was. I do not totally condemn this: the country might be better off if everyone showed the same enthusiasm for their work. It was serious, though, when a concussed jockey rode before completely recovered. Not only was he a danger to himself, but worse still a danger to other riders. The system is a good idea, but not yet foolproof. On several occasions after being knocked out—and once breaking a collarbone—no entry was made in my book enabling me to ride again if I wished without prior examination. The last time this happened was at Ascot and because it was the third time I made a stink about it in the press. I was, of course, making trouble for myself as far as racecourse doctors were concerned.

In November 1974 I broke a collar bone eight days before Lanzarote was due to run at Ascot in a valuable race. The entries were poor and the race looked in the bag. The broken ends of the bone were pulled into place that evening by Alun Thomas, a Mayfair osteopath, who then fitted leather rings around each shoulder, fastened together by tight straps, forcing the bone to stay in position. He phoned his Swindon counterpart John Skull who agreed to treat the swollen area with an ultra-sonic machine to disperse it, allowing fresh blood to flow to the broken bone. John treated me twice a day and on the sixth day gave me permission to ride at exercise. Fred Winter, whose loyalty was to the owner, and to the lad who looked after Lanzarote agreed that I could ride him the next day if I proved myself fit by riding a novice entered for the first race of the same afternoon.

There was only one thing now to stop me; I must be passed fit by the racecourse doctor. The Ascot doctor had been hurt by my remarks in the papers and was sure to give me a rigorous examination, which no doubt I would fail only eight days after the bone had been broken. The rules were definite; no blue ink clearance, no ride. The answer, when it hit me, was so simple; go to another meeting and be signed off by the doctor there. Duly accomplished I presented myself 'fit to ride' at Ascot the following day winning on both the novice and Lanzarote, netting £245 as my 10 per cent present. It had worked! No bone actually mends in that time, and although I was fit to ride I was not fit to fall on it for some time. There were, of course, all sorts of ways of cheating which one by one were uncovered. The first was to show another rider's book for clearance, carefully keeping a hand over his name. This was stopped when a nervous jockey dropped his borrowed book to reveal its true owner's identity. Lads then reverted to several other dodges which, when discovered, were squashed by large fines on the guilty parties. My opinion is that the scheme is a good one only if enforced to the letter, which means fines also for medics who fall down on their part.

There is sometimes a lighter side to injury. On one occasion I was at Perth Races, riding for Major Bewicke's chief patron, at that time, Lord Cadogan. His horse Fashion House, a very headstrong fellow, was ten lengths clear as he approached the penultimate fence when without warning or reason he ran headlong through the running rail giving us both a nasty fall. I was knocked unconscious and my left shoulder was dislocated. This injury is more painful than a break because it is a 'ball and socket' joint where the ball has been wrenched out of the socket, tearing all the sinews, tendons and muscles apart. I came round in the ambulance, my left arm out of sight and almost severed from its moorings, supported by a kindly Scottish member of the St John Ambulance Brigade. After an

'Ouch, that must hurt!'

The Queen Mother is one of the great race-course personalities. Meeting her was one of my greatest moments

A world closed to outsiders. Valet Joe Ballanger tends to the jockeys' needs

Fred Winter and myself developed a great rapport

The entire team: Mr and Mrs Boucher (owners), FW (trainer), Me, A. Brown (lad), M. Cullen (travelling head man) and Killiney (horse)

Sheer joy is written all over my face after winning the Champion Hurdle, 1973

Another great success, Jasper completes his 450th victory

Lanzarote. *Above:* a classic hurdle jump; *below:* not so classic

The original Fred Winter team

It wasn't all glory

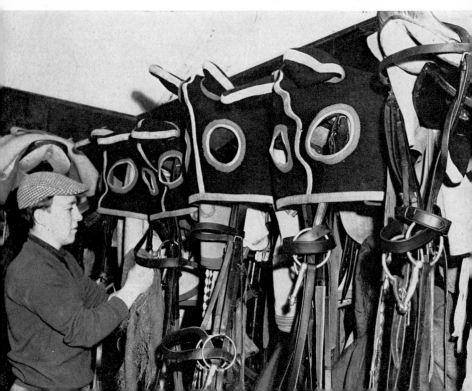

Killiney jumps high over the open ditch at Cheltenham – Tote Champion
Novice Chase

I could always be recognised by my thighs – Charlie Potheen wins the
Hennessey Gold Cup

Jumping Bechers Brook. Eddie Harty, Me and Tommy Carberry neck and neck

Pendil (No. 4) takes the open ditch for the last time before going on to win the King George VI Chase at Kempton Park in 1973

examination by the course doctor, I passed out again.

Hurried plans had now to be formed by Major Bewicke. A replacement jockey must be engaged for the next race which was due to start in seventeen minutes. Lord Cadogan's first thought was for my wife who would be waiting anxiously by the phone for news of the day's events, good or bad. Injured riders are taken by ambulance six miles out of Perth to a good hospital at the Bridge of Earn. The hospital doctor tried in vain to wrench the joint into place whilst I was conscious, so he ordered an anaesthetic to be administered.

I loved the sensation caused by the injection: it seemed to start from my toes, slowly enveloping my whole body with a warm sticky feeling. As it reached my head I was floating amongst little puffy clouds, warm and snug with not a care in the world. On waking several hours later, although it felt like seconds, I was in a state akin to drunkenness. My immediate action was to pick up the phone to speak to Jenny.

It transpired that the Major in his excitement had forgotten Lord Cadogan's request to phone Jenny. My words were slurred as I spoke and as I had been expected at Heathrow airport several hours before Jenny assumed that I had been drinking.

'Where the hell are you?' she demanded. 'In the Bridge of Earn,' I replied. 'Well, come out of that pub immediately. Your dinner's dried up in the oven and I'm furious.' It took several minutes to get the true facts through to her, but she finally realised what had happened. I flew home the following day to be met at the airport by a tearful wife. I was still in a state of concussion. This was a severe bout which lasted for three days during which I slept for long periods. My waking hours were unpleasant for everyone, I was irritable with Jenny and my two sons and could not walk four paces before I lost my balance and stumbled. I would not hear of any treatment until Jenny, besides herself with worry, telephoned Fred Winter knowing he would be able to persuade me to have my head examined.

There was no lasting damage that time, but it made me

C

think how serious it could have been. Every summer since then I have seen a neurologist who checks the condition of my skull and its contents. I realised that I could do without most limbs and organs, but not without a working headpiece. My fears have been unfounded and the fact that my memory is not perfect is due more to complacency than to wear and tear. The neurologist always asked questions before making a graph from the impulses my brain sent out under varying circumstances. This was obtained by placing twenty electrodes on my scalp which recorded every move my brain made. To me, a layman, it looked like any other graph, but to the professional it showed my reactions to calm, excitement, light, darkness and surprise. Concussion was a frequent entry in my medical record book, so much so that I was warned by the Jockey Club Medical Officer that if it continued I would be advised to stop riding.

This was the deterrent I needed and from that day on, as I left the saddle to go into orbit the 'Gypsy's warning' flashed through my mind, and as I neared the ground I tucked my head into my chest, rolling over on one shoulder. I suffered no more concussions. Instead I either broke my collar-bone or dislocated my shoulder!

This leads me to a situation that I felt very strongly about. Several jockeys have been stopped by the Levy Board surgeon from ever again riding in races because of minor brain damage. When the Jockey's Association tried to obtain compensation for loss of livelihood the Levy Board made a case for normal wear and tear. The battle for fair play waged for some months before the Board finally agreed to pay the Jockeys their compensation. I was adamant that brain damage bad enough to stop a jockey riding was not normal wear and tear. In my case it led to a premature loss of both hair and teeth and the acquisition of a deeply furrowed brow.

The worst damage I have done was to break an ankle in three places in a fall at Sandown Park on 12 March 1971. Shortly before the race I was interviewed by John Rickman on the television about my prospects for the remainder of the season, having ridden forty-eight winners at that stage and being only three behind the leader, Graham Thorner. I said that the next race would be number forty-nine, that I would win the following day on Vital Sanction and had nine fancied rides at the big March meeting at Cheltenham the following week. It will be seen that I did not heed the saying that 'Pride comes before a fall.'

There were only three runners, my horse being the favourite. As the race progressed my horse jumped better each time he met one of those formidable Sandown fences until at the last of the 'quick' three fences he started to tire slightly.

I could hear a rasping noise coming from his throat and realised that the operation he had undergone for breathing trouble had not been a success. Not wishing to punish him unnecessarily I accepted defeat and decided to jump the last three fences behind the two leaders. He met the penultimate fence too far to stand off. His next stride took him right to the base of the fence, forcing him to twist in mid air to clear it. This sudden twist caused my saddle to catapult me out of the 'side door', landing on one foot which naturally could not stand the strain. It cracked with a sickening noise sending severe pains shooting through the nervous system. There were no other horses behind me to do any damage and I had landed like a paratrooper, yet I had sustained my worst injury. Ironically it was a simple fall compared to the crashing falls and kicks from the hooves of thirty-horse fields that I had endured so many times before and yet been able to stand up immediately. I had done in fact the same as someone jumping from the roof of a car travelling at thirty-five miles per hour and trying to land on one leg.

I have never feared falling although I dreaded the thought of being 'hung up' and 'dragged' after a fall. Usually as a horse falls, the jockey is thrown from the saddle, his feet coming free from the stirrup irons, terminating the partnership. But occasionally a rider's boot at the moment of impact goes through the stirrup iron, twisting around as they thrash about on the ground and is imprisoned when the horse gets to its feet. If the rider is conscious at that time he can, if he is quick enough, grab at the reins before the horse gallops off to pull him round in tight circles until a helper comes to the rescue. Some horses, feeling the weight of a body caught in the stirrup iron, will not chase the other runners, enabling the jockey to extract his trapped foot. The dreaded situation is when the horse sets off after the other runners and feeling the strange burden, panics. With each stride he pulls his victim underneath his hooves, kicking and cutting with his steel shoes, his half-ton weight behind each blow.

I have only seen this happen once and God forbid I should ever see it again.

My first ride at Aintree was on Darting Legend in the Mildmay chase. He fell at the farthest point from the Grandstand where Jenny was watching the race through her binoculars. The commentator said 'Darting Legend's fallen at that one . . . he's up on his feet . . . but he's dragging his jockey.' Jenny's reaction was understandable: floods of tears, panic and a headlong flight down the stands to the course. Had she waited a few seconds longer she would have heard it announced that I had disengaged myself and was lying thankfully on the wet ground breathing great gulps of wonderful fresh air.

I was brought back by the course ambulance which suddenly came to a halt amidst a lot of shouting and argument. When I asked what the trouble was the attendant told me that 'A damn fool woman' was hysterical in front of the ambulance. It was, of course, Jenny who was unyielding to the driver's plea to get out of the way. They eventually got the message and let a now near to collapsing Jenny into the ambulance with me. Jockeys' wives (or rather the wife of a jockey) suffer far more than the jockey himself because they live in constant fear of their husband not coming back, whilst the jockey knows the extent of the damage straight away. A few wives become hardened to the job and can be seen following a race through binoculars, pausing only momentarily as their husbands do several somersaults and crash to the ground.

Mrs Irene Dewhurst, one of the nicest owners I have ridden for, had a novice chaser called Loon, which I thought a great deal of. His schooling at home was faultless and his gallops were impressive, but his record on the track was five races and four falls, of which two really hurt me. Mrs Dewhurst wanted the guv'nor to sell him before he did any lasting damage to me, but I would not hear of it. I had so much faith in Loon I would have ridden him at Aintree. In his races I would set off towards the rear of the field, giving him plenty of daylight at the obstacles, jumping with confidence and never putting a foot wrong. When the race had settled to a pattern I would allow him to improve his position, passing several of the more moderate jumpers and staying within striking distance of the leaders. Our undoing always occurred as I unleashed my challenge at the penultimate or the last fence. Loon, full of running, would jump with speed consolidating his new lead only to fail to put his legs out and once again we would roll over together.

The actual fall happens very quickly. One second you are sailing over a fence at thirty-five miles per hour, the next you are both rolling on the turf. When a jockey hits the floor the noise is loud, the breath is knocked out of you and you roll into a ball as the rest of the horses go over your huddled body, most giving a fleeting kick as they pass. At this point the noise seems deafening as some strike your helmet and those that do not hit you depress the ground all about your head. The silence that follows as the field fades into the distance is sweet indeed and the friendly voice of a watcher saying, 'You can get up now dear, all is clear,' is more than welcome news.

Falls are a part of the job, but punters' reactions vary as their money clouds their judgement. On one occasion at Plumpton, having won on two horses already I was approaching the second last fence well clear of the other runners when, hardly rising at all, my mount crashed to the floor. The impact caused my helmet to come over my eyes in doing so breaking the bridge of my nose and sending blood all over my face.

Graham Thorner, who had been standing at that fence, helped me to my feet and accompanied me back towards the weighing room, but as we drew level with the cheap enclosure an irate punter leaned over the rails and grabbed me saying, 'Is that all that happened to you sonny?' For the few pounds he had lost he did not want blood, he wanted bones as well. The other side of the coin was once revealed to me at Windsor races. Having fallen when in the lead at the last fence, the whole field seemed to play football with my helpless shape, leaving me really battered about twenty yards from where I had landed. I jumped up to be greeted by howls of laughter and one cockney shouted out, 'Who's a pretty fellow then?' Never having been noted for my good looks I was puzzled by this, but glancing down I saw to my dismay that one boot and the whole of my breeches and tights had been ripped off leaving me exposed to the world and his wife! On another occasion at Windsor I suffered a crashing fall. Black Plover, my mount, was owned by Mr and Mrs Rex Boucher, who at that time were quite new to racing. Having seen the effect my fall had on Jenny, Mr Boucher vowed that in future he would provide for any jockeys who rode for him by insuring them privately in addition to the meagre £15 a week that the Levy Board paid at that time to injured jockeys. He did so, but taking it much further than that he pioneered the present scheme whereby owners are compelled to pay £2 per ride into an accident insurance run through the Jockey's Association paying £35 a week for temporary disablement.

10 *Racecourse characters*

One of the delights of racing are the characters that can be seen almost daily on the racecourses. During my early days as a jockey I met very few of them because as soon as I had finished riding there was work to be done in the stables before setting off home in the horse box. When I became a fully-fledged rider I either went with my trainer or drove myself, and was thus at the course with time to see things that go unobserved by the occasional racecourse visitor.

There has been for many years a small, very old Jewish gentleman usually known as Nadie. He lives in London travelling to every meeting covered by British Rail, no matter what the weather or time of year. Nadie is by no means a fair weather punter. He can be found occupying a position somewhere between the complimentary entrance and the weighing room with two bags of lucky sweets. Nadie knows everybody who makes a regular trip to the weighing room and, always smiling, passes the time with pleasant chats, never asking for a winner but delighted if someone says, 'Have a few bob on mine today Nadie, it worked really well yesterday morning.' As the first race approaches he will scurry off to the paddock, then to the bookies (delighted to relieve them of their money) and will always be present to clap the winner into the enclosure. This man should be an example to us all because I have never heard him speak ill of anyone. He always pays his entrance money with a smile on his face and simply enjoys life.

The younger element is headed by 'Dodger', so called because he dodges around the bookies seeking out favourable odds for his bet, which can be quite considerable. He is a professional gambler and will be seen at steeplechase meetings somewhere in Britain every day that racing is held. He drives a yellow, open-topped E-type Jaguar equipped with a first-class radio and a portable television as a means of keeping in touch with the racing scene. On Friday evening in Newton Abbot after racing Dodger, who oozes charm, was seen chatting up a girl with a view to taking her to the races the next day, but on the next day there was no Dodger to be seen. It transpired that after reading his *Sporting Life* at 7.30 a.m. he spotted a 'good thing' in the 3 p.m. race at Fakenham in Norfolk and promptly set sail, a distance of 260 miles from bedroom to bookies. I don't know if his good thing won, but I dare say he was able to make the journey worthwhile by noting a future winner.

I was told by a Jockey Club security man that being seen talking to Dodger was unwise, because people would assume I was betting, something punishable by loss of licence to ride. I thanked him for his concern but said that I would continue to talk to Dodger if the occasion arose. He never asks a jockey for information because it is well known that they are the worst tipsters. On the contrary, if Dodger said I would win on a horse I was pleased because it confirmed my evaluation of the form.

In any case, there is no information to be got from Fred Winter's yard because everyone of his horses is trying to win each time it races. During the ten years I rode for him I was never asked not to win on a horse. Each horse ran on his merits, although the Guv'nor would not have a horse whipped just to win a race; he thought much too much of his horses for that. His instruction before a race would be, 'Give him a chance early,' (i.e. not too close to the leaders) 'put him in the race two hurdles from home, give him one reminder with your stick to let him know you are serious, then ride for home with hands and heels.' He might pause for a second then add 'Even if it's a short head do not hurt him.'

Men who make their living by betting are very rare indeed. They must study the form book inside out and watch every race that they have not wagered on to see horses that will improve the next time. Horses improve for many and varied reasons. The most common reason for improvement is when a horse has not been 100 per cent fit. The benefit of a race will bring the horse on ten lengths or more according to his physical condition and mental makeup. You may argue that horses should not run until they are completely fit, but this is not always possible.

A young horse for instance, having been broken in, schooled and then galloped, will still be quite a roly-poly individual. Since birth he has done nothing except eat and four years later has an abundance of fat about his frame. His training will reduce the fat, turning much of it to muscle, but in order to get him fit first time on a racecourse the trainer would have to gallop him so much that his forelegs would not be able to stand the strain. His first appearance on a racecourse will do as much good as three weeks galloping at home, yet the strain is minimal.

The morning of a race starts with a lead down the road to stretch his legs, no hay on his return to the stable and his mane being plaited. This drastic change from normal routine makes all but the most stupid horse realise that something is afoot, and when his legs are bandaged before being loaded into a motor horse box he begins to worry a little. The racecourse itself is a mass of noise, colour and continual comings and goings, making our newcomer shake with nerves or sweat with excitement. The race is so different to the orderly procession on home gallops that the animal can easily lose a hundredweight in body weight or surplus fat as nervous energy.

If the horse finishes fifth or sixth on his first outing you could normally expect him to be fighting for honours next time. But he may be very backward and need three or four races to bring him to peak fitness. The exceptions are horses who are of an excitable nature. First, at home exercise they do everything with twice the effort that the lazy horse does, becoming fitter much more quickly, and they will probably run really well first time out. Here the inequality of the sexes plays its part. A filly often runs very well on its nerves first time out, but goes to pieces next time, whereas a nervy gelding will last for several races before needing a lay-off period.

The careful punter looks and decides what sort of horse each one is and then watches them carefully, deciding which if any, will win next time they race. He will also need to know their breeding to judge what will be its best distance or what type of going will suit it. The seasoned performers run each year to the same pattern; some always win first time, others need the sun on their backs to put them in the right frame of mind and some only win at a particular course. So all in all a punter's life is a precarious one, and to last at the job a punter must also be a character who can accept Lady Luck's decisions.

Travelling down to Lingfield Park once on a crowded race train, the buzz of chatter was suddenly broken by a loud, continuous barking. There was no dog in the carriage, but one chap in particular was making a fuss about finding it. The man turned out to be 'Chick', a retired entertainer who amongst many other talents possessed the art of ventriloquism. Chick, like Nadie will be stationed on the well-worn path to the weighing room, armed with packets of smoked salmon for those who stop to pass the time of day with him. He also never asks for tips, but probably hopes for some glint of information to emerge from the conversation. During racing he can be heard barking amongst the bookies, or seen tap dancing on the members' lawn, delighted by a captive audience.

These people share in common the friendship of every jockey and most of the leading trainers. Fred Winter, who usually has at least four runners each racing day, and their respective owners to entertain, never passes these racecourse characters without saying a few words to each. There is also a man who manages to pop up in four different guises most racing days. He can be seen on arrival in the yellow uniform of the National Car Parks, directing cars to a safe parking place, then a visit later in the day will find him assisting at the Jellied Eel stall, this time with a white coat covering his frame. On leaving the course he will be stationed at the exit playing bright tunes on his well-worn accordian, and really late leavers will notice the same man picking up litter on the racecourse. The days that the regular paper sellers fall ill or fail to turn up he will also be seen selling the *Sporting Life.* A greedy man? No. Just a man not afraid to work hard enough to support himself. It is a pity that those people who are content to live off the dole don't take a leaf from his book.

Given space I could fill a book on racecourse characters alone. There are the car park attendants, cheery in all weathers; the fish stall proprietor who sells a side of smoked salmon to successful owners and cockles to losing punters; there is the famous Jean who sells liquor to celebrate with or to drown your sorrows; the gatemen with their unending tales of glory or woe on foreign battlefields; the jockeys' valets, who live and work with us for ten months of the year, and probably know many jockeys as well as the jockeys' wives do. I am glad to have known them all.

11 *I like people*

To return to my own story: My career was taking shape in the 1967–68 season, my eighth year as a professional jockey. I decided that I needed to be known by more trainers and permit holders and so I determined to make two new acquaintances every time I went racing. At first my approach was quite wrong. People were not interested in my nervous blurted introductions and a quick resumé of my limited achievements. However, I did meet a permit holder who was more than willing to talk in great detail about himself and his horses. This was the obvious way to go about my mission; a quick 'How do you do', and congratulations on their recent winner or how well their horse had jumped. I never actually asked for rides but hoped that when my new acquaintances were looking for a jockey my name would be lurking in the back of their minds.

After a very short while I realised that I was not putting my carefully-made plan into operation, but doing what interested me most, meeting people. Jockeys who telephone owners and trainers for rides are frowned upon by their counterparts and called 'telephone jockeys' but although I never had cause to telephone for rides I admire a man who does. It is a business. A man's livelihood is at stake, and it is a poor sort of man who sits at home getting fewer rides each year but congratulating himself on the fact that he never rang up for rides. After all, as Bill Shand-Kydd told me three years earlier, 'A man can only say No, he can't bite you.' Godfrey Burr, a local farmer, who has kept racehorses about his farm for many years and supported most of the local claiming riders when they make their bid for recognition, asked me to ride his horses when

72

available. (At that time I was very available.) Godfrey gave
me many rides and several years later gave Johnny Francome
his first winner on Multi Grey at Worcester. However, I had
one less lucky experience. One rainy Saturday at Chepstow I
rode Multi-Power for Mr Burr, who was unable to come racing
because of a Church Meeting. The horse, as his name suggests,
was very strong.

The only reason men can control strong animals is because
we have better brains than them and can fool them. Multi-
Power was not only stronger than me, but also far cleverer.
He plunged forwards the moment he felt the turf below his
feet, catching me sitting relaxed with yards of rein in my
hands. Every time that I caught hold of him during his headlong gallop the wrong way round the course he quickened
again and pulled the sweat-covered reins out of my numb
fingers. We approached the other runners who were standing
at the start at a full gallop and to my delight Multi-Power
deciding that he had finished teaching me a lesson, pulled
himself up. The starter asked if I thought he was in a fit
condition to run. I replied that he was, at the same time
thinking that it was me who was in no fit state.

The race was a normal novice hurdle except that my steed
and I knocked down six of the eight hurdles in the race. We
did, in spite of that, come with a storming run to lead on the
finishing stretch and take the spoils. When the blood started
to pump around my veins again and I had time to go over the
day's events I suspected that Godfrey had probably gone to
the Church Meeting to pray for our safe return!

That season also saw my introduction to a formidable
woman trainer, Mrs Barbara Lockhart-Smith. It is probably a
hard life training racehorses, a man's world, and they do say
that attack is the best form of defence. She certainly did that.
In fact she described our relationship as a 'love-hate' relationship, we argued so much, we loved to hate each other would
have been nearer the truth. I was able to see her good points
though there were racing people who could not. Mrs Lockhart-
Smith was to my mind, a very good trainer of racehorses, but

there is more to the job than training alone. Most successful trainers are liked and respected by their owners who race because it is an outlet from a hectic business life and an enjoyable way to entertain your friends. The Lockhart-Smith establishment was in the tiny village of Cublington, a peaceful hamlet near to Leighton Buzzard in Bedfordshire. Peaceful that is except on schooling mornings, usually on a Sunday.

It would start for my wife and me with a two hour drive from Lambourn. The moment we stepped out of the car the trainer would try to overpower us with a barrage of orders, 'Richard we're all behind, just give them a hand to finish mucking out.'—'Tony, *Tonee!!* You know I want those bloody dogs shut up.'—'Oh Christ, has that child fallen out of the damn window again?'—'Jenny be an angel, cook the breakfast while we are schooling.'

Jenny and I had not driven two hours to cook and muck out for the mistress of The Manor House, Cublington, so a conflict was inevitable. The schooling session would proceed eventually, with much crying and gnashing of teeth and the return to the stables saw a mentally tired bunch of people. A hurried breakfast prepared by everyone was followed by a planning session with occasional references to several owners who had braved the elements. This usually ended by the champagne being circulated freely amongst all present resulting in owners and jockeys going home in a far better frame of mind than they had been for the previous three hours.

It was on one of these schooling mornings eighteen months later that Jimmy Drabble, a new owner, was persuaded to buy his first racehorse. Mrs Lockhart-Smith knew it could be bought reasonably and was qualified to run in the Grand National. In fact this particular horse won for them in Ireland two weeks after purchase and went on to be second in the Grand National. More of that later; the horse has yet to run in the 1968 National and figure in my story.

Race days were just as hectic, whatever the result, something would be wrong. If you were fourth you should have been third, third and you should have been second, second you should have won and if you *won* you had won too far or not far enough. At the time it was hard to swallow, but in retrospect I believe she thought it the right thing to do; and she could certainly train racehorses. We had many successes between us, her horses always looking well. Most racing folks would deny that she was soft-centred, but occasionally her defences were lowered for a brief moment. After winning a three mile hurdle with a sprinter at Ludlow, owner, jockey and trainer went to the bar to celebrate where after the usual fumbling in her handbag she would ask me for a loan of a £1. To my great surprise she didn't use it to buy cigarettes, instead she quietly moved to the far corner of the bar and gave the £1 to a poor old lady whose job it was to clean out the ashtrays. I like genuine people and Barbara Lockhart-Smith had shown me that day underneath her fiery exterior there was a lot of kindness trying to fight its way to the surface.

The terrible Foot and Mouth disease struck again that winter adding another hazard to the sport and its dependants. Major Champneys gave me my first ride since those far off days when my head was in the clouds, on Domaru at Wincanton where he was a course specialist. The race was well within his scope but he trailed around finishing a very tired last. At least, that is how I interpreted his performance. The Major thought differently, for when I dismounted he uttered one sentence, 'He pulled your leg Pip.' I had to accept it when he won his next outing in the hands of Tim Norman, and it hurt.

That season saw my first meeting with Her Majesty Queen Elizabeth the Queen Mother who took my heart by storm. She represents to me all that is good in life and everything that a mother and grandmother should be. I do not intend to expound her greatness because my pen is not fit to do so, but I will tell you that it was my burning desire above any other racing honour to don her racing colours for a race when she would be present to watch me ride.

The first time I 'bumped' into Her Majesty was at Kempton. I had spent some time in the course hospital recovering from concussion and as I wandered back to the weighing room trying desperately to remember what had happened, I came to the winning enclosure. I walked with stooped back and a bowed head until before my eyes were a dainty pair of pastel blue ladies shoes. I slowly raised my head until my eyes met the owner of the shoes, it was to my surprise the Queen Mother. My scrambled brain was slow to operate.

'Oh . . . err . . . Hello,' I stammered as my eyes opened to the size of saucers. Her Majesty smiling sweetly said, 'Good afternoon young man, I think you ought to sit down for a while, and please do not drive to your home.'

Her Majesty has several steeplechasers in training and is by no means a fairweather owner, she watches her horses all through the winter whenever her duties to the country allow it. On the occasions she has presented me with a trophy after winning a race, or chatted for a while at a cocktail party, it has increased the burning admiration that I have for Britain's leading lady. The ovation after Her Majesty's Tamuz had won the Schweppes Hurdle at Newbury was indicative of racing folks' esteem for her. And at the same time when Lanzarote beat Tamuz in the Welsh Champion hurdle, she was the first person to congratulate Fred Winter, Lord Howard De Walden and myself.

There was one man who I liked as a person but who continually got in my hair in racing matters. Eddie Harty was first jockey to Fred Winter while I was second, and although at that time I was first jockey to Major Bewicke, Eddie was beginning to ride the odd fancied horse for him. When the long list of entries for the Grand National narrowed down to the final acceptors, Fred Winter had two horses to run, Steel Bridge was Eddie's choice and Manifest was my ride. Steel Bridge had run in the Grand National on three previous occasions, completing each time without posing a real threat to the leaders, while Manifest had never been to Aintree and was not the best of jumpers of ordinary fences.

On the morning of the race after the final gallop Fred Winter took Eddie and myself to one side and said he thought we would finish the race close together as there was little between the two horses. For the first circuit Manifest was able to lay up close to the leaders as we 'hunted' round just trying to survive. Eddie's green and white check colours were always in my sight. I was determined to beat him at Aintree where the men are sorted from the boys. Manifest jumped far better than I had expected, adopting a style of his own. He respected these formidable fences, realising that to treat them lightly would invite disaster.

As the survivors start on the second circuit every rider reverts from huntsman to jockey, the initial test passed. My arch-rival's colours slowly drew further ahead of me as Manifest failed to answer my call to quicken his pace. At the third last fence with the leaders well beyond my reach I realised Eddie had accepted defeat and was riding to get round, which is itself a feat. This was the moment I had waited for; at last I would outride him. The Grand National was almost over but *my* private race was just beginning. I summoned every last ounce from Manifest as with each stride Eddie's back came closer until, landing over the last fence, we were level.

Eddie glanced casually across, saw the determined expression on my face and rode for his life! The whole length of that agonising run-in, which has seen so many battle-royals, witnessed yet another one, only this time the contestants were tenth and eleventh in the actual race! Each rasping breath felt like boiling oil as it was forced into my lungs and amidst loud cheers we crossed the line still locked together, both convinced we were ahead! The *Sporting Life* showed that Eddie had triumphed yet again by a head. Would I never get him out of my hair?

In fact the following year I finished second in the Grand National on Steel Bridge. Where was Eddie then you may ask? He won it!! To cap it all, although I was now riding a lot of winners I could feel my position with Major Bewicke becoming shaky with Eddie riding more than just the odd fancied runner for the Major.

I met another man that year who has remained a real friend through thick or thin. He was and still is a genius with a camera, always clicking away in the right spot at the right time. I was going through a period of falls at the London Park meetings—Sandown, Kempton, Ascot and Lingfield—and sure enough, each time as I picked myself up, there, camera in hand, was this enormous tousle-haired man grinning from ear to ear. After my fourth fall in six days we introduced ourselves and chatted at length about racing photography. Gerry Cranham studied courses in detail before selecting a spot which would provide the action, and his unwilling accomplice for the previous six days had been me.

Gerry does a lot of work for the major public companies like Shell and Players so when he described me as a 'floater' I challenged his right to criticise me in a sport that was new to him. He explained that a 'floater' was a jockey who did not grip with his knees when jumping a fence. I did in fact, grip with my ankles, wearing out racing boots within a very short time. Gerry produced a photograph to illustrate his point and I humbly include it in this book. The thing that did amaze me was Gerry's power of observation when looking through a camera lens.

Most racing folk cannot read a race properly: that is to say they do not see its real contents. They will be convinced that a losing jockey is brainless because they could not interpret the circumstances he encountered. My riding career has been a happy one not only through winners but because I have enjoyed meeting and talking to people. In racing circles even the rogues are likeable ones.

12   *I had arrived*

In the 1968–69 season I was still with Major Bewicke, although my position at first jockey was decidedly shaky. Eddie Harty was still riding a lot of fancied horses for the Major and remained a thorn in my side. Bobby Beasley was then first jockey to Fred Winter. To watch Bobby school was an education.

At that time the trend was to ride with short stirrups adopting a style like our flat counterparts. He showed real artistry riding with very long stirrups. Never would his hands be above the horse's withers nor his back other than horizontal. Bobby was a part of his mount not an adition to it. Although he was the best retained jockey that Fred Winter had secured, it was evident to me that his severe weight problem and temperament would not suit the set up for long. Was this to be my chance? It was my ninth season as a pro and I had now ridden forty-four winners, still not exactly a Fred Winter or a Josh Gifford, but I was at least holding my own.

Major Champneys gave me another ride, Coturry, a sister to Domeru. I made sure that she didn't pull my leg, winning easily at Fontwell Park. That win gave me great satisfaction because I had always felt that I owed the Major a lot for my grounding. Plumpton had put on an evening meeting and Lifeboat, trained by Fred Winter and ridden by Josh Gifford, was one of the winners. He was also declared to run at nearby Lingfield Park for a race the next afternoon and after close examination the Guv'nor decided he was fit to take his chance. Josh had to ride for Captain Price in the race so I was given the ride on Lifeboat.

The morning's torrential rain was right against my steed

and Josh, knowing that he had given Lifeboat a hard ride just eighteen hours before, grinned at me like a Cheshire cat. Fred Winter had walked the course formulating a plan as he went along.

'Stay on the inside for the first three hurdles, leaving yourself room to edge to the outside flight for the next two where the ground is best,' he told me in the paddock. 'When you start down the hill pull right off the hurdle track, cross the chase course until you hit the public footpath. The ground is firm there and the lengths you give away to start with will be worth it by the time you head for home.' I thought the Gov'nor had really flipped this time and Josh's remarks as he walked by didn't give me much encouragement.

The race went as planned until I headed for the footpath and saw to my surprise and horror that Josh had beaten me to it. I stayed close behind him and sure enough we forfeited our position ahead of the field who to our delight, were beginning to flounder in the mud. Having got their second wind our horses skipped down the hill overtaking horse after horse until we headed for home five lengths clear of the field. Josh took a quick look over his shoulder and seeing it was me tucked in behind him, allowed himself a grin of satisfaction.

I know the feeling so well as certain victory is turned suddenly into defeat, but this time it was Josh who felt the draught as Lifeboat and I swept past him to a length win. That win meant a lot to me in terms of experience: the race had been won by one horse and nearly won by another because two trainers had walked the course while lesser men were entertaining in the box. It was only a fortnight later that walking the course paid off for me and any punters who happened to back Vintage at Fakenham. My pre-race inspection of this little Norfolk course revealed an unusual feature: the winning post was forty yards *after* the end of the grandstand. Vintage was trained by Barabara Lockhart-Smith who had done well to keep this bad-legged horse sound enough to race. Coming with his usual late challenge Vintage was fully eight lengths behind the two leaders as they rose together at the last fence. The leading jockeys both stopped riding as they reached the stands, looking around for the winning post, which was, of course, not there. Riding like a man inspired I drove Vintage past the bewildered jockeys to get the spoils. It was the first time I had *pinched* a race!

It is my opinion that bad jockeys throw away many races that they ought to have won, but good jockeys only steal several races each season that they should not have won. This is because, given equal oportunities, there is little to choose between the top twenty-five riders, but the less talented jockeys leave much to be desired. In my opinion the jockeys who win races when riding a moderate horse against a good one are, at the time of publication of this book, Graham Thorner, John Francome, Jeff King, Ken White and Paul Kellaway from the south, Martin Blackshaw, Ron Barry, Tommy Stack, Gerry Griffin from the north. There are also several older jockeys who steal races through sheer experience and cunning on really moderate horses. Unfortunately, because Joe Guest and Jimmy McNaught ride bad horses with 110 per cent of effort and ability they get earmarked for horses in this category and overlooked for the best grade horse which quite often could be victorious with my Aunty Edith in the saddle.

A little race at Catterick on 19 October 1968 produced a small bay horse called Pendil as the winner. His time was 9 seconds better than the average, the start of a prolific career, always 'better than average'. Fred Winter did not see that race but when he came up for sale six months later, secured this equine star-to-be for £3,600. At the time when Pendil was winning at Catterick, there was a race 200 miles south at Newbury which would sort out the best four-year-olds of that year. I was then in favour with Fred Winter and so had the ride on Soloning, a £500 purchase. The two proven young-sters were Fred Rimell's Coral Diver and Major Cazalet's Escalus ridden respectively by Terry Biddlecombe and David Mould.

Races are always good to ride in at Newbury because the

track is almost two miles around and there is plenty of room to manoeuvre with a long finishing straight.

The race progressed like any other until approaching the second last hurdle the three above mentioned horses drew clear of the pack. David Mould had the inside berth on Escalus, I was beside him and Terry was on the outside. All three horses were galloping flat out as we approached the last hurdle, who ever jumped the best would win. They rose as one, not a semblance of a mistake betwen them and it was every man for himself to the winning post. Under pressure, Soloning hung towards Escalus and had we bumped the race would have been lost in the Steward's room for sure. Not having room to pull my stick through to the side that was nearest Escalus, I sat still for two strides until he returned to an even keel, then with hands and heels I rode for the winning post making certain that Soloning was balanced for the last thrust that would get his head in front.

It did. The photo-finish showed Soloning the winner by a short head from Escalus with Coral Diver a head away in third place. To David and Terry it was just another race, slightly annoying to be so near yet so far, but still only another race. To me sitting in my corner of the changing room it meant the turning point of my career. My finish had always been the weak link in my make-up as a jockey but that day I had not only held my own, I had won. The significant thing here was having beaten them once I had a newfound confidence. I felt I had arrived.

I was keen to pick up different jockey's attributes and adopting those which appealed to me. Stan Mellor was a great thinker before he did anything. He would sit in the changing room looking at a wall or a window for fully five minutes until suddenly his problem resolved itself. His reply to my question was as I thought it would be. He said that before a race he would block his mind off from the banter all around him and try to picture the shape of the race to come. He would run and re-run the contest until a plan covering all eventualities had been formulated in his mind's eye. When a split-second

decision was needed, Stan found that having rehearsed every
situation his subconscious leapt into action immediately.
Another trick of his was to count out loud the last three strides
before taking off at a fence. This had the effect of destroying
other jockeys' concentration, sometimes forcing them to make
a mistake. Every jockey measures up the strides to each fence
as soon as he has a clear view of it. He tries to ease back or
push gently forward until three strides away from the fence
when the rider mentally counts to the take off giving an
encouraging kick or flick with his whip on the third stride.

Stan's counting out loud would put his rivals at a dis-
advantage when they were on number two stride and he
shouted three. They would unwittingly tighten the body
slightly, causing the horse to think it was the signal to take
off.

Taffy Solomon also tried a similar piece of professionalism.
When his mount was on its take off stride Taffy would shout
'Huw . . . p!' causing several other horses to take off too soon.
These little tricks only work for a while and then the thinker
must think again. Another thing that puzzled me about Stan
was when in a tight finish in heavy ground he would pull his
horse off balance for a stride and then quickly pull it back
into its proper stride. If an aspiring jockey did such a thing
the scribes would be down on him like a ton of bricks and
his trainer would cease to give him rides. Stan's reasoning
was that when horses were really tired in heavy ground they
needed a mental jerk to wake up, so if they thought they
were falling the brain would snap to attention long enough
to produce the winning energy.

13 *Return to Uplands*

I ended the 1968–69 season with thirty-three wins to my credit, finishing with a good run of successes to prime me for the start of the 1969–70 season. After two rides Bobby Beasley decided the continual fight against increasing weight had taken its toll. He retired, only to return four years later to win the Cheltenham Gold Cup on Captain Christy and—having been a self-confessed alcoholic—poured celebratory champagne for all his fellow jockeys without one drop passing his lips. I had driven him home from Fontwell the day he decided to finish and I would have laid long odds that he would never ride again. He was in a distressed state after the race, unable to sit on his bench, with eyes sunk deep into his head his laboured breathing was gasped spasmodically. We left the course an hour after his race and when we drove into Lambourn another two hours later, Bobby's condition was little improved. His rapid increase in weight was encouraged by liquid intake and drastically reduced by a handful of dehydrating pills taken on the morning of the race.

Bobby's sudden departure left Fred Winter without a jockey and to my joy he asked me if I would like to take the job. I was still contracted to Major Bewicke as first jockey and after considerable thought decided not to go through the unpleasant procedure of severing our partnership at that time. It had been five years since first I joined the Guv'nor at Uplands and it was a further two before I had the job to myself—not exactly meteoric fame! Paul Kellaway was asked and accepted the job as retained jockey to Fred Winter with me as second. My share grew as the season progressed.

The season provided me with wins in two big races, the

Great Yorkshire Chase on Freddie Boy and the Whitbread
Gold Cup on Royal Toss. Both races gave me great satisfaction,
for very different reasons. Freddie Boy could most kindly be
described as a character. He needed to be kidded along
in his races, never going too near the wing of a fence, or he
would run out, nor taking the lead until after the last fence
because he would stop racing if in front. Like Charlie Potheen
he also had a dislike of righthanded tracks or ones without a
running rail for company. Doncaster provided everything in
our horse's favour; a left-handed course complete with running
rail and good ground ensuring a fast-run race which would
enable me to settle Freddie Boy in the bunch until delivering
our challenge going to the last fence.

Fred Winter had done his homework with his usual zest
and was proved right. Freddie Boy won the Great Yorkshire
Chase handsomely. The second big race, the Whitbread Gold
Cup, is the last major chase of the season. Being run in April
or early May the ground is usually firm. It is a handicap, the
best horse having to carry 12 st. and the worst 9 st. 7 lb. It
is usually a very fast-run race because of the ground, and the
lower weighted horses make sure of a good gallop to tire the
high weighted horses. Tim Handel, a farmer-trainer, had given
me the ride on his horse, Royal Toss because his usual partner
had been badly injured several months before. At halfway we
were nearly last and not making much headway, but then as
the hotheads up front felt the effects of the fast pace they had
set we slowly made ground on them. It was hard work as
inch by inch Royal Toss ploughed on in his relentless pursuit,
but swinging wide of the tiring leaders we swept to the front
to win. The Sandown Park racegoers are well known for their
ovations and Royal Toss's connections got their due.

It is a marvellous feeling to be lifted on the wings of
applause but a jockey must never wallow in his glory for too
long. The same crowd will want his head on the block when
he rides a losing 'good thing'. The Queen Mother presented
Tim Handel and myself with our trophies, a proud moment
never to be forgotten by us. It is customary for the winning

owner of a major prize to send a case of champagne into the changing room for the riders to share the victory with. I looked for Tim but he had high-tailed it back to Somerset, not being interested in the remaining races, which were on the flat.

I ordered a case of champagne myself and duly shared it with the other jockeys, both flat and jumping, until none was left. A week later I went to Tim's home to pose for the local press and before leaving I presented him with a bill for £47 for the champagne I had bought on his behalf. He looked thoughtful for a minute then said, 'No, Richard, half those jockeys were flat boys who would never ride for Tim Handel the farmer, they'd be much too grand. And the jump jockeys that were there would never ride a school after racing for me. They are your friends so you pay the bill.' I admire him for his action and the thought that went into his decision. Too many people do things for effect or because it is the thing to do. Tim was right and had the courage of his convictions.

That very same man showed me his metal four years later when my car broke down in Taunton at 11.30 p.m. I had to get home that night and the last train had left Taunton Station an hour before. At midnight I phoned Tim Handel, who without question got out of bed and fetched me to his home where a steaming hot drink had been prepared by his daughter. Without further ado he put his car keys in my pocket and told me to take his Mercedes Benz. Actions like that are priceless and very rare. The 'downs' always come before and after the 'ups'.

Twice in the eleven years I was associated with Fred Winter I received a 'roasting' after a race. Both occasions were in 1970. The first one came when I was riding Sonny Somers at Cheltenham. He was a strong little character who like Freddie Boy needed to be held up for a late run. On the canter to the start Sonny Somers came very close to taking charge of proceedings, giving me a taste of things to come. Casting my eyes over the other runners at the start reassured me that given normal luck we would beat off any challenge that they could offer. The Starter's assistant checked the girths and

signalled to the Starter that everybody was now in a fit
state to start. 'Walk slowly up boys,' he shouted, but his
command fell on deaf ears. It seemed that the riders had all
been given orders not to go on at the start. A situation I did
not want. Because of the riders' reluctance to 'go on' the race
was run at a very slow pace, enabling Sonny Somers to fight
for his head right from the start. Each hurdle was an excuse
for him momentarily to get the better of the battle for freedom, because on soaring over an obstacle a rider loosens his
grip on the reins to enable the horse to stretch himself. The
really headstrong horse takes advantage of this action, and
before the rider can gather up the reins, the horse steals a
march on his partner.

By halfway, every muscle in my body had reached its limit
and a fantastic leap on the downhill run took Sonny Somers
into the lead. The damage being done I decided to let him
run, hoping to steal ten lengths whilst the rest were playing
cat and mouse. It worked and, allowing myself a glance over
my left shoulder as I spend towards the last hurdle, I saw
only one horse coming in pursuit. On landing Sonny Somers
looked up the long finishing hill and decided that as there
were no more obstacles in sight he would take it easy. My
urgings were of no avail. He shortened his stride enough to
allow the only challenger to draw level and finally beat us.
Fred Winter was aware that I had thrown the race away and
before I could open my mouth to explain he barked his dis-
pleasure in front of the gathering crowd. It was the first time
he had done so and it hurt. The car journey seemed long due
to the stony silence, broken only by intermittent statements of
fact.

'You knew at the start they would not go on.' 'Any one
with brains would have got left a few lengths.' 'The last
would have been early enough.' 'Christ, I wish I had been on
his back.' I did not reply to any of this. Instead I mentally
rode the race again with different tactics, and of course a
different result!

The second time I received the rough edge of his tongue was

only two months later at Sandown Park on a great old favourite called Beau Champ owned in partnership by several film directors and Hayley Mills. Again the same situation arose at the start. Every jockey hung back from the starting gate until the Starter shouted, 'Jockeys, if you don't come into line I will fine you all a tenner.' Beau Champ had fallen on his last three outings over fences and had been entered in this hurdle race to restore his confidence. The orders were, 'Win if you can but get him round in one piece and do not be hard on him. He always gives his all. And enjoy yourself.'

Bearing this in mind, and not wishing to be fined a tenner, I lined up in front of the dallying jockeys. I set a moderate pace over the first four hurdles with Beau Champ not taking a great hold of the bit, but as we turned downhill away from the stands he set sail, catching me by surprise. His jumping was as good as any champion hurdler, with each leap taking him farther away from the rest of the horses and his headlong rush then completely out of my control. We entered the home straight fully thirty lengths clear and then as if he had been shot, Beau Champ slowed to a canter to be passed on the run-in by four horses.

On returning to the unsaddling area my eyes met the Guv'nor's, which had narrowed to steel-grey slits. His voice was not much more than a whisper, but had a real bite to it. 'Get off that horse. You'll never ride him again. Be at the car in five minutes.' Again the homeward journey was made longer by the icy silence. After dropping the Guv'nor off at Uplands I drove deep in thought to my home ten miles away. Jenny met me at the door with a message to return immediately to Uplands. It was with great trepidation that I walked into Fred Winter's study, to be confronted by a smiling boss who put his arm around my shoulders and escorted me to a seat.

'Have a drink, Richard,' he said brightly. A very large gin was placed by my chair and the Guv'nor then explained why he had been so angry. It transpired that he could not bear to see a horse finish as tired as Beau Champ had done, it would put him back for a month not bring him on as was expected.

To a great jockey, as Fred Winter had been, it must be very hard at times to watch men who do not possess his skill, performing on horses he had trained to perfection. These two occasions were the only times he reprimanded me for race riding. He is exactly the same in victory and defeat as the photographs of Pendil's short head defeat and Lanzarote's victory show.

I finished the 1969–70 season with thirty-four wins making a total of one hundred and two winners. I had three major races to my credit and was now satisfied that I had arrived. The season ended with a split between Major Bewicke and his principal owner, Lord Cadogan, after fourteen years together. It also ended my association with the Major and left me free to share Fred Winter's job with Paul Kellaway.

14   *A hive of activity*

By the start of the 1970–71 season I had become a prominent figure in the weighing room. Many of the old heroes had retired and a new generation of jockeys was feeling its way cautiously.

There are four major valets licensed by the Jockey Club to look after the jumping boys wherever they ride. Their job is to lay out their clients' silk colours, along with a pair of breeches and racing boots, and ironed neckerchief, crash helmet, whip, goggles, string gloves, and elastic bands to hold the silk sleeves neatly to the arms. They help to dress their jockeys, prepare saddles with the correct weights and girths (short, medium and long) add breastplates or blinkers and generally pamper their clients. The master valet employs as many helpers as he thinks necessary to supply a good service to his jockeys. The master valet in the North, Phil Taylor, still gives a complete service to his jockeys and loses money annually rather than reduce the quality of his work.

Unfortunately in the south, through old age, retirement and, in one case, affluence, the service provided really went downhill until the jockeys themselves persuaded John Buckingham to retire from riding and start valeting. With a guarantee of support from four prominent riders, the Jockey Club granted a licence to John and his partner Buster Rooney, who was also an ex-jockey. This action met with stiff opposition from the southern valets whose monopoly was about to be broken. The desired effect took place, and although friction existed to begin with it is a fact that once more a good service was resumed in the tiny rooms where jockeys and valets share fluctuating fortunes every half hour.

A jockeys' valet must leave home hours before the jockey himself in order to arrange clothes and equipment for as many as forty riders. Each jockey will want attention through the day as if he is the only man there, and the changing room echoes with cries of, 'John, where's my clean gloves?' 'Never mind him, my race is first'; 'Buster I told you the fourth ride was to be ready early. Where are his blinkers?'

At the end of the day, when the last jockey leaves the room, a glance over his shoulder will reveal a mountain of mud-caked boots, saddles and fittings and the whole place looking as if an army had passed through. On a wet day, as much as four hours' work remains for these men before everything is washed, dried and the saddles oiled. Mechanical aids are often minimal and the hours long. If you ask any valet why he does the job, it's hard to find the answer.

On arrival a jockey will greet his rivals like long-lost pals even though they have done battle the previous day. He may have a chat to his trainer about the plan of campaign, and then a quick game of cards to relax. There will be several jockeys under extreme pressure: an owner may have £2,000 on his horse to win; or perhaps, unless the jockey can manage to scrape a winner that day his job will be lost; or it may even be that the horse he rides in the novice chase is positively dangerous. Laughter and action are the remedies for pressure of that kind, and the changing room becomes one continual comedy show.

In the North the merry band of jockeys consists of Martin Blackshaw, Gerry Griffin, Tommy Stack and Pat Buckley, with Paddy Broderick and Brian Fletcher supplying their own brand of humour. In the South, Johnny Williams, John Francome and Taffy Solomon are the practical jokers with David Sunderland and John Buckingham pouring forth a continuous flow of verbal jokes.

Sabotage is the most common entertainment. If I was riding for a very curt trainer who lived only for racing, I would check my saddle carefully before handing it over to him. One of the boys might have removed the girth straps or shortened the stirrup leathers to such a degree that the horse would try to throw me in the parade ring. Johnny Williams lives near Swansea and so has a lot of time at the wheel each day. He spends much of his driving time thinking up practical jokes for when he finally meets other jockeys. An early trick of his was to find someone who had several rides in succession. While they were being rushed off their feet he would place a tomato sandwich in the roof of their helmet. The moment that it was put on, squashed tomato would ooze out on all sides of the victim's face. Tiring of this trick, Johnny would eye the excited jockeys who were watching a televised race from some other meeting and, satisfied that they were sufficiently pre-occupied, disappear into the adjoining canteen. When he reappeared he was holding a cream bun. He would walk towards the jockeys and pretend to trip over a saddle, extending his hands as he stumbled, depositing the cream bun all over Phil Black's face. Profound apologies were accepted until the same trick was repeated four minutes later and retreat was the only course then open to Johnny.

Most loos in the changing room are of the half cubicle type, i.e. open at the top. Often when jockeys don't want to talk to difficult trainers they take the *Sporting Life* into the loo and spend twenty minutes contemplating. Before a novice chase, when nerves run high, the loo is a much frequented place and the only way to flush a jockey out (if you will excuse the pun) is to throw a bucket of cold water over the top; the result is immediate evacuation by the surprised occupant, complete with a soggy newspaper. Another favoured plaything is the diuretic or dehydrating pill. Placed into a 'friend's' cup of tea it produces remarkably quick results. Lead weights heaped into an overnight bag causes loss of temper when a jockey is trying to beat the post-race traffic.

These and many other harmless juvenile tricks, coupled with the continuous flow of jokes, make the dangers of the job seem far away. The riders are always busy between races, oblivious of their friends' problems until it dawns on a jockey that his adjacent colleague's clothes have been hanging limp

right: A great horse – the head of Killiney

below: Another great horse – Crisp at the Parade of Champions, Wembley, 1975

left: Taking a bend – Me, Phil Blacker and Richard Smith

below: Pendil studies his own reflection in the water jump at Kempton Park

right: You can see here why Gerry Cranham labelled me a floating jockey

below: The photo-finish to the 1973 Cheltenham Gold Cup, with The Dikler taking Pendil by a short head

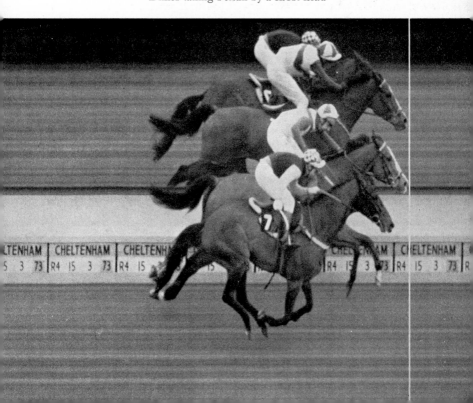

Teaching a two-year-old to jump

The 1973 Grand National. Crisp clears the Canal Turn well in front of the field

bove: The 1973 Grand National.
The end of a *great* race

right: My biggest disappointment –
no – the thrill of my life. After the
1973 Grand National

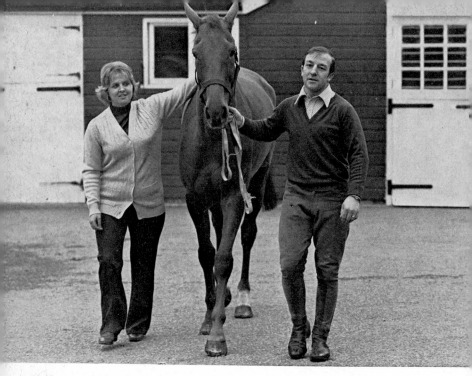

Our first racehorse. High Tide won two point to points for us in 1973

Larbawn on holiday, being ridden by Eric Wheeler

'What's happening over there then?' Paul's bribes are rejected!

A man of leisure!

Contentment

on his peg for several races. He could be in the shower; but, no, there are no crumpled silks or muddy boots. A shouted enquiry to his valet reveals that Joe broke a thigh two races previously and has been taken to hospital. A general chat between the lads ends with one volunteering to take his injured pal's clothes to the hospital and, if things are not too serious, drive him home.

Only jockeys and valets are allowed into the actual changing room, which is the heart of the weighing building. There are many doors leading into it from various other rooms but the changing area is out of bounds to others: it is the jockeys' sanctuary.

Most jump jockeys do not place high regard on their clothes and turn up daily with the same brown trilby, suit and overcoat. David Mould is the exception, a smooth dresser. He appears in the latest fashion, meticulously cared for, and hangs them up with loving care. Meeting head on at Cheltenham he ran his eyes over my attire and after several shakes of his head, said, 'Rich, let me have £500 to play with and I will dress you properly.' Then, after several seconds' deliberation, he added, 'No, on second thoughts, don't bother, after a week you'd look just as you do now.' David is also immaculate when he enters the parade ring: his breeches and boots are perfectly tailored, a pair of white gloves is tucked neatly into his breeches tops and the silk cap is always secured squarely on his helmet.

On the other hand, conforming with the tweed suit and trilby brigade has never been Ron Atkin's forte and, because of this, his riding chances have been limited. He dresses according to the latest fashion and, when long hair became popular, Ron was the first to follow suit. His riding is first-class, but because he has the strength of character to say what he thinks is right and to do his 'own thing' his opportunities have been limited. Ron is the jockeys' spokesman on racecourse safety and takes the job very seriously indeed. Although not welcomed with open arms by racing's governing body at first, he is now listened to and respected.

D

As in the army regular jockeys get to know each other as well as, or even better than, their wives do. It is apparent that even though some may drink too much or others may be slightly promiscuous each and everyone is a solid character, to be relied upon completely.

Several years ago riders who were too heavy for a fancied ride were able to cheat at the scales when weighing out. They were of course cheating themselves, but would consider the horse capable of winning even with the extra three pounds or so. This practice was stopped by not allowing jockeys to go back into the changing area after weighing out until they had given their saddle to their trainer in full view of the Clerk of the Scales. The most popular method was to weigh before the race with a tiny, paper-thin dummy saddle, go back into the changing room and substitute one suitable for a big chaser. After the race, when the jockey had to weigh back, a clever explanation was needed to avoid being fined or cautioned. On hot days, when riding a lazy horse, it is possible to lose a couple of pounds in weight during a race. This was indeed welcome when a little cheating had taken place, but embarrassing when it had not. The rules allow a rider to weigh in two pounds under the allotted weight, but more than that means that the race will be awarded to the second horse.

It is my belief that the now defunct cheating was the lesser of two evils. Most chasers win quite easily and would do so with several extra pounds on their backs, and although weight brings horses together it is only the low weighted horses that were affected by this action.

On the other hand, if a jockey is determined at all costs to 'do' the correct weight he will run hard, go to the Turkish baths and finally take a physic. The result is that the jockey is so weak that he is a hindrance to his horse instead of a help, forfeiting any chance they might have had. Another reason for not condemning this 'cheating' is that if a horse hits a fence hard it probably ruins its winning chance: A healthy and alert rider is far less likely to make a mistake than a weakened shell of a man who has over-dieted. So you should not frown too hard upon the increased number of overweights you will encounter; it may be in your favour.

The weighing room in 1968 was the first place that I saw multi-coloured pills being used willy-nilly. We are now in an age of injections and pills for every ailment, but at that time to see several leading jockeys swallowing a green pill followed by a white one intrigued me. I was very soon to learn all about the pills, their uses and effects. The curiosity that killed the cat led me to inquire about them, and the best way to find out was to sample one of each colour and size.

At that time I had no use for such aids but I was to call upon all of them several years later. The physic pill is used to empty the stomach of all its contents, leaving the recipient feeling not only empty but very low. The physic can be taken either by a tablet called Regulot or in chocolate form, named 'Ex Lax'. Both are taken the day previous to the race day for which the rider must lose weight and necessitate many trips to the lavatory during sleeping hours. It is unpleasant but effective.

There are two unpleasant side effects. The first is rejection by the body of the tablets or chocolate and after a while it is necessary to force them down with a glass of whisky, or a similar strong-tasting liquid. The second is that the system gets used to their power and the dose has to be increased each time. One Regulet would lose three or four pounds from a normal person, but a fairly successful flat jockey took thirty-two tablets in my presence when he was an apprentice in order to move his bowels.

The result was horrible. Mother Nature realised what damage would be done and made him violently sick. He retched long after his stomach was empty. He was too weak to ride the following day. Now he is riding a continual flow of winners without the help, or perhaps hindrance, of the physic.

A totally different aid is the pill which takes away a man's appetite, obtainable from dieticians in most major cities. I was recommended to see a doctor in London. After a thorough examination he gave me a diet to follow. He stressed the need to cut out alcohol, extra salt, and starchy foods such as bread, potatoes and sugar, and to limit my milk intake to a quarter pint a day, either taken all at once or in cups of tea or coffee. I was to eat three times a day, my diet consisting of lean meat, fish and eggs. When asked about my diet on television, my tongue-tied reply was, 'Mish, feet and egg,' to which the interviewer smilingly added, 'tasty although the feet are slightly indigestible!'

The doctor insisted on hard-boiled eggs for breakfast because they contained 50 calories but needed 100 calories worth of energy to digest them. The briefing was followed by an injection in the backside and two boxes of coloured pills to be taken each morning before 7 a.m.

It amused me while sitting in the waiting room to try to analyse the other occupants and their reasons for wanting to lose weight. Most were models or actresses trying to keep their figures and their jobs, and the rest were businessmen who wanted to lose their beer bellies. The treatment worked and my weight tumbled down but, as with most other methods, there were side effects. Hard-boiled eggs tasted like cotton wool, fillet steak was boring, and fish really turned my stomach. The pills that should have made me not want to eat did so because they were amphetamine. They made me walk on air, high as a kite. The pills were so strong that if not taken by 7 a.m. the patient would be wide awake until dawn when he would come back to earth with a bump, feeling depressed and in need of more to lift his spirits. My journey into cuckoo-land did not last a single day after my wife realised what was entailed.

The third type of pill that used to be part of the weighing room scene was a diuretic called Lasix, the latest and most effective one ever devised. Its function was to force the kidneys to work long after their natural work had finished. Twenty minutes after swallowing one Lasix the user passes water and does so every ten minutes for an hour, tailing off to three times during the second hour. Depending on how much excess liquid the body was holding the amount of pounds lost varied considerably.

My first venture with Lasix, on the way to Towcester race-course, forced seven stops before I dried up, some of them in a state of panic. The result was that in the space of sixty miles I had lost eleven pounds and felt like death warmed up. I rode in six races that day, winning two of them. But I felt like a rag doll when I finally slumped into my car for the homeward journey.

A peculiar side-effect was that I could hear my words inside my head as if it was a cave, instead of from the mouth to brain via the ear. Cramp was another unpleasantness to be tolerated if the benefits of the pill were called upon. I tried to keep Lasix as a last resort in case a fancied light-weight ride came my way on the morning of a race, but, like all other medicines, in the end one pill would not even make my eyes water!

A lot goes on in the weighing room that may be frowned upon by certain parts of the community but it is a hive of activity where your own problems are always overshadowed by your mates' disasters, and where most of the alliances formed last long after the right to enter is lost. Of the double handful of *true* friends that I have, most are housed in the weighing room.

15   *Five golden years*

From 1970 to 1975 my dreams came true. I had the out-standing luck to be associated with a team of truly great horses. Each year provided bigger and better thrills and the winners increased both numerically and in importance. At the beginning of those years, the names of Pendil and Bula were unknown except to Vince Brookes, the young man who had charge of both of them. Pendil ran fifth first time out for Fred Winter, before streaking home by twelve lengths a week later; and much to everybody's surprise Bula bolted in on his debut. The latter's win illustrates just how hard it is to pick a winner from home gallops, because he had shown no sort of spark when working except on the occasions he schooled over hurdles. The Guv'nor secured Stan Mellor to ride him, because Paul Kellaway was hurt in the previous race and I was nattering as usual far from the weighing room.

Fred Winter's orders were to give the horse a nice race, coming with a challenge at the last hurdle to win, after a pause, 'if you can'. Bula won all right. In fact he won his only six races that season and was not headed for sixteen consecutive races after that—not bad for a horse that could not win an argument at home. His record at the start of the 1975–76 season is twenty-nine wins from thirty-seven starts.

I only had the pleasure of riding him six times, five times a winner and once on the floor. He was the first of Fred Winter's cluster of stars. Vince, his handler and regular rider, knew his every mood, so much so that the Guv'nor confered with him before a race to see if any unusual sign was visible to him. A horse will reveal his well-being or otherwise to his handler in many ways that a trainer or headman would pass over as unimportant. Vince rides Bula and Pendil nearly every day at exercise, a responsibility I would not care to have: both horses are lively characters who pull hard on the gallops and prance about on the slippery roads. The comments in the *Sporting Life* about Pendil's debut read, 'Nearest at finish, better for the race'. How right they were! He won six hurdle races and was only seven pounds below top class in this sphere.

Like so many National Hunt horses Pendil 'got a leg', in his case in the Schweppes Hurdle of 1971. His main tendon was operated on by the Lambourn Vet, 'Spike' Kirby, and nine months later Pendil made his winning debut over fences.

This goes to show just how much of a team job racing is, with each link bearing its own importance. The head man is responsible for the feeding and general welfare of each horse. The lad must devote his attention to care for his charge's every need. The veterinary attends to the finer internal workings and the blacksmith needs to be a foot doctor. The jockey ventures his post-race opinions and finally the captain of the team, the trainer, collects the information from each member before putting it in perspective.

When Pendil had recovered from his split tendon operation the Guv'nor decided I should school him over fences, thinking the slightly slower pace of a chase would compensate for any speed lost by ageing and the operation. The result was breathtaking. Pendil floated through the air, taking off a stride before his schooling companion and landing as far the other side of the fence. The second and third fences were treated with the same contemptuous ease, a thrill that could not be bought, it had to be earned. Trotting back towards the Guv'nor my whole body tingled with excitement and anticipation of things to come. Trying hard to conceal his delight Fred Winter told me to go over the larger fences to show Pendil that they were not toys to be treated lightly.

Giving him the freedom of his head, he relaxed as we walked back to the starting point for the second school, but the moment I started to gather up the reins he became a coiled spring just waiting to be released. In the few seconds I held him still I could feel his heart pounding and the rushing blood forcing the veins in his neck to protrude through his shining coat. His gait changed to a gallop immediately I 'let out a notch' and, treating the larger fences as though they were hurdles, confirmed that he was out of the ordinary. Ed Byrne captured Pendil's big jump through his camera at Kempton Park and the caption the *Sporting Life*'s correspondent put to it was 'Poetry in Motion'.

My remaining five glorious years hinged on Pendil, Bula, Killiney, Crisp and Lanzarote, which proves the old saying that 'Good horses make good jockeys'. The short journey from the schooling ground to the stables was filled with ambitious plans for our new-found chasing star, culminating with the Cheltenham Gold Cup. The Guv'nor had seen horses flatter only to deceive many times before, but this time permitted himself to share the dreams of Brian Delaney, Vince Brooks and myself. The proud owner-breeders in Ireland while annually showing him their young horses, had pointed to many a handsome colt saying, 'Sure, that's the one for you Fred, it's going to win the Gold Cup'. So although he secretly had great expectations of Pendil, Fred Winter would not verbally commit himself. Whenever he makes a statement you can be sure that a great deal of thought has been behind it.

The third of our nap hand was Killiney, a strapping great horse 17.1 hands high. He was an absolute Christian in every respect, earning the nickname of the 'Gentle Giant' from his owner, Mrs Enid Boucher. Mrs Boucher and her husband Rex were new owners in Fred Winter's yard, having one other horse, Grey Cavalier, a winner, but one who lacked the ability to go to the top.

Mr Boucher was a tenacious and successful businessman who made it clear that he wanted a champion. Little did we know that with only their second horse they possessed a novice with unlimited potential. His size and gentle character could easily have labelled him as an overgrown, immature weakling, needing the age-old remedy of time, and lots of it. Paul Kellaway, who had the pick of the rides, asked to be released when Killiney made his debut at Ascot, in order to ride River Rother, a winner of its previous race, so Killiney became my ride by chance.

I have been criticised by betting people for exposing a young horse too much and Killiney's first run was ammunition for them. On his first racecourse appearance, starting at 20–1, he was overlooked by all the shrewd betting people. But were they shrewd? Fred Winter's horses were always run on their merits and what I lacked in ability I made up for in determination.

My way of introducing a young horse to racing was to start half way down the field, giving him plenty of time to get used to the hurly-burly of the race and letting him see each obstacle clearly. At the half-way stage of the race the excitement caused by the unknown diminishes, enabling me to collect my steed and put him amongst the leaders. Once in the firing line he must hold his position at each obstacle and, if he is fit enough, go on to win. In Killiney's case, when I put him into the race proper at half way, he took hold of his bridle and pulled me to the leaders, battling right to the winning post. Unfortunately there was one horse too good for him on that day and we finished second, but the race had shown that with normal improvement it would take a very good horse to lower his colours in the future. In fact the Gentle Giant went on to win six of his seven hurdles races that season, finishing with the Players No. 6 final at Chepstow.

Paul's decision to ride River Rother instead of Killiney provided me with the ride which I kept for the duration of his career, which shows just how much luck plays a part in the career of a steeplechase jockey.

That same season the Australian champion chaser arrived at Uplands, via America where he finished fifth in the Colonial Cup. The journey right round the world and a tough race in America had taken its toll on Crisp, who on arrival looked like an enormous hatrack. The Guv'nor could see further than this great shell: 'Just look at the depth of his chest. He must have a big heart in there.' When asked about his plans he replied 'None just yet. Let's get some flesh on him first.' It was in the middle of the winter, which proved to be a new experience for Crisp, who had never know cold weather before. Besides being very suspicious of snow his coat grew to almost unknown lengths within a fortnight, making him look like a hairy hatrack.

As soon as he arrived in the yard he was commandeered by Chippy Chape, an Englishman who had spent several years in Australia as a jockey and knew Crisp's capability. Chippy has looked after him with great devotion ever since and like Vince Brooks has ridden his charge in most of his home gallops. He was the subject of leg-pulling every day, because Crisp bore no resemblance to a racehorse at that time; and also the lads loved to have a go at someone who took the bait.

Chippy would defend his hero to the death if necessary and several mornings came close to it. When Jumbo Heaney tried to clip Crisp's coat both he and the clippers came out of the box far quicker than they went in. Crisp had never needed to be clipped before and he most certainly was not going to accept the 'mechanical fly' that was tickling him now. After several futile trys, an immobilising drug was used to complete the clipping, only to reveal a silky skin and a lot of new muscle acquired since his arrival. An infra-red lamp was installed in his stable and two under-blankets added to his night-rug to compensate for his lost coat.

The training muscled Crisp so quickly that he took a great deal of steadying on work mornings. Galloping with his head down, Crisp tested Chippy's strength, bringing sweat to his brow and a satisfactory smile to his face. It was with great expectations that the team went to Wincanton races for Crisp's English debut on 11 March 1971 where a large crowd gathered to inspect him in the parade ring. He had been allotted the burden of 12 st. 7 lb. to carry, which he did with contemptuous ease. Crisp jumped fast and accurately to take the lead three fences from home.

Going to the final obstacle he was travelling so fast I could not visualise him being able to get his legs out in time to land. He did, and a rousing cheer accompanied him to the winning post where I had the devil's own job to pull him up. He covered the two miles over twelve jumps in the record time of 3 min. 55 sec. (The record only stood for six months before Fitzcard beat it, but he was carrying 2 stones less.)

The lads were silent the next morning, allowing Chippy to wallow in his deserved glory and delighted that the stable housed another star. My own personal dreams were smashed along with my ankle the following day at Sandown Park as told earlier. It was only five days later that Crisp won the two mile Champion Chase at Cheltenham by twenty-five lengths as I watched him from my hospital bed. Paul Kellaway completed a great double by winning the Champion Hurdle on Bula. Now the stars were really shining.

The fifth member of the group, Lanzarote, was still racing on the flat, a game that he had been bred for, but he joined the Fred Winter stables at the end of the season to be schooled ready for the following campaign. Paul rode him during his first season in which he only ran twice, winning at the second attempt. Looking back now, Fred Winter worked miracles to get him regularly into condition. The horse was always dry in his coat and suffered from back trouble.

Again, as with Killiney, Lady Luck played her hand in my favour with Lanzarote. At the start of the 1972–73 season I was finally made first jockey to the Uplands stable with John Francome as my depute. Lanzarote was to be his ride. He ran two respectable races before going to Ascot when he finished second to Windrush. It was anybody's race from the last hurdle to the post. Unfortunately for John the chink in his armour was a weak finish, so the mount was given to me. He won his next race unchallenged and was subsequently unbeaten that season. Had John been given just one more chance I would never have put a leg over Lanzarote. But the penny has turned a full circle, and now I have retired he has the ride again.

These five stars headed the successes that came my way

and by creating confidence in my riding helped me to better my total each year until the last season. My record for the total seasons read as follows: 0–0–0–0–3–7–12–24–33–35–48–59–84–79–46—my five wonderful last seasons make quite a contrast with the first five!

Right from the start I loved race-riding and never considered the hours involved, the ever-present danger of injury and the relatively small financial rewards. Throughout the last five years I often thanked my lucky stars for being paid to do a job which was also my pleasure and I was aware that no matter how wealthy a man was he could not buy the thrills that were mine, provided by these five superstars. It is said that success breeds success. I wholeheartedly agree, for when I had a good winning run reactions were quick and accurate but during a succession of hard luck races the subconscious thought twice before activating my limbs.

In 1972–73 I had thirty-one winners at Kempton Park alone. Whatever I did was correct, and every meeting provided at least a double—a far cry from my first four years without a single winner, or the depressing run of eighty-six consecutive rides without getting my nose in front.

Many changes are brought about by success. When the chair for the Jockey's Association became vacant I was voted in, not realising quite what it entailed, although I am now pleased by the education it provided. A National Hunt jockey becomes so obsessed with steeplechasing that everything else is ignored. My newspapers were only opened at the racing page and at social events restricted to horsey gatherings. Being chairman of the association meant attending many meetings at the Jockey Club and Levy Board offices, and had the jockeys not had Major Peter Smith as secretary and guardian this particular country boy with egg on his face would have been swallowed whole.

It was quite awesome the first time I sat at the oval conference table along with another thirty or more representatives of every section in racing, but the sound of my own voice spurred me on and quite soon I enjoyed speaking on behalf of the jockeys. On one occasion at the Levy Board offices lunchtime came long before the current problem had been resolved, and everybody trooped off to a nearby hotel.

The chairman of the Levy Board at that time was Lord Wigg who tried to put us at our ease by telling us to have whatever we fancied. A quick glance at the menu brought me some relief, for amongst the 'starters' was Vichysoise soup. I had ridden a horse of that name for several seasons although I had never even seen the soup before, and the correct pronunciation was known to me. Not wanting to appear too backward, and also trying to impress my colleagues, I immediately called for Vichysoise to start with, Dover Sole to follow —resisting the urge to ask for it 'rare'. When my soup arrived I was aghast to find it was cold, and revolted when I tasted it. One spoonful was enough for me. I wished I had ordered a conventional soup, so to cover up I talked my head off to his Lordship through the first course. Just before Lord Wigg finished his smoked salmon he spotted my untouched dish and asked 'What's the matter with your soup, my boy?' 'Not up to its usual standard, my lord,' I quickly replied. He promptly snapped his fingers and ordered a fresh bowl of Vichysoise for me and watched in silence as I consumed every horrible spoonful. I learned my lesson and accepted that I was a country boy after all!

I also learned from these meetings that although politicians and high-ranking officials are very honourable men their knowledge of our mother tongue enabled them to turn my words to suit their own cause. The answer was, of course, to play the same game, which I enjoyed doing immensely. I have been present on many Jockey Club enquiries and believe that justice is done in nearly every case, although I am convinced that a known rogue is sometimes found guilty on a dubious charge when a previous blatant offence has not yielded sufficient evidence to pin him down.

Having said that I must correct the balance. At least twice I have seen innocent men found guilty of a charge when I knew that they were, on that occasion, innocent—while I knew them to have been guilty of previous breaches of racing rules.

Jump racing is as straight as it can be, and in the fifteen years I rode I was never asked by any owner or trainer to do anything to stop a horse from winning. On one occasion as I walked to my car after racing at Sandown a large black-haired stranger walking beside me said it would be worth £1,200 to me not to win on Pendil in the Arkle Chase at Cheltenham four days later. When the full meaning hit me I stopped at once, looked the man in the eye and told him I was going to report him to racecourse security. He vanished immediately into the rushing crowd and I have never seen him since. Pendil won the Arkle Chase and I received my 10 per cent of the winnings, which came to £342. I glowed with pride as I entered the winner's enclosure to the cheers of thousands of happy racegoers. Money, and especially crooked money, could never have bought the feelings that moved me that day. In any case my truest assets were honesty and loyalty to Fred Winter and the owner: if I threw those away I had nothing. Of course, I have known cases of horses being 'stopped'—but, ironically, the horses who are pulled are the ones which would not have won anyway.

16 My fellow jockeys

For six days a week, almost ten months of the year we jockeys ride against each other, drive to and from race meetings together and socialise in our own company. It would almost be true to say that I know my fellow jockeys' characters as well as their wives do. Every chink in their armour is revealed and irritating habits grow out of all proportion, mine included.

The bulk of the jockeys change with regularity. Each year boys get a chance to make a name for themselves and for a multitude of reasons do not make the grade. The sheer weight of numbers of would-be jockeys means that few mistakes are tolerated before a boy is passed over in favour of the next in line. The lads that do make the grade usually stay on top for a decade before younger jockeys topple them from their perches.

Of my friends who are jockeys Graham Thorner is first to come to mind. He started as an amateur jockey being supported by his father who farms in Somerset, and soon made his mark in that sphere. It wasn't a case of a wealthy man buying his son into racing, in fact it was quite the opposite. Mr Thorner is a working farmer, who sent his son to Tim Forster to see if he was good enough to make the racing game his living. He provided enough money to pay Graham's weekly lodgings and a £1 to spend on himself, which he never did. Graham knew from the start his capabilities and, without any big-headedness, expected racing to need him, but had the good sense to realise the importance of advertising his wares.

Of the eighty rides he had in his first season, Graham got seventy-five himself, his trainer supplying the other five. Within a very short time Tim Forster recognised his worth and used him to his advantage by turning him professional. He quickly became champion jockey, and promptly won the Grand National on Well To Do. These two things out of the way, he relaxed slightly and started to enjoy his racing, but still devoted himself totally to everybody who employs him. If efforts could be measured in money Graham Thorner would get £40 per ride instead of the £17.50 earned at present. And although he has a reputation of being a hard jockey he can when necessary be as sympathetic as the best to his horses.

I have always sat on the fence slightly and admired the way Graham refuses to let go when he believes in something. One day at Hereford, when he was very much a junior, Graham thought he had won a race by the length of a horse's head until, walking back to the winner's enclosure, he heard the other horse's number announced as the victor. He refused to believe it and to the embarrassment of his connections kicked up an almighty row until an official said 'Thorner, the judges decision is final, and photographs do not lie.' Under duress he succumbed to the wishes of his owner and trainer and quietened down.

On his way from the weighing room to his car he passed the board where the prints of the photo-finishes were posted, only to have the fire inside him rekindled. It quite clearly revealed that Graham's horse had won! About turn and back into the Stewards' room he went, and producing his evidence to the surprised and angry officials: surprised that this young whipper-snapper had not gone home and angry because he was right.

'The judges decision is final,' roared the Senior Steward, but Graham was not put off that easily. He threatened to send the print to the newspapers, and caused so much fuss that the stewards agreed to refer to London. Graham had the bit firmly between his teeth by that time and would not go home, so he booked into a local hotel to see justice done.

It was. He was awarded the race and drew £27 as his percentage of the prize. It was not even enough to pay his two days' expenses, but he had not done it for financial gain, he had done it because he knew he was right.

He always seems to be rushing whatever time of day it is. The fact is that he is a grafter whether it be at exercise, driving, racing, or on his forty-acre farm. On the rare occasions he sits still he even needs to watch two programmes at once on the television with the aid of an automatic switch.

As he is such a hard, factual man it is hard to believe that he is superstitious, but he is. Anything that was used when winning a big race, is lucky, in fact sacred. Graham still rides in a pair of blue underpants, full of holes, which he wore when he won the Grand National, Now they are so holey he has to wear tights over them to keep them intact. Whips, saddles and articles of clothing have their lives extended if they happen to be present at the winning post on special occasions. Trains passing under a bridge that he is crossing make horses win, chimney sweeps are lucky, two magpies flying past, and even a funeral, are welcome sights on a day Graham has fancied rides. He is a man who likes to fight for his successes and is afraid of no jockey from the last fence to the winning post. He revels in a flying finish and hates to be congratulated for winning a race easily, feeling that he has not earned it.

In my opinion he is wrong on this score because although the end might have been easy another jockey would have ridden an entirely different race, probably running into trouble. To the victor goes the spoils. Graham Thorner is an honest man and, without being a churchgoer, he is my idea of a Christian. I believe if I asked him to take me to John O'Groats he would do so without question.

Another jockey of equal standards though much more placid is Willie Shoemark, who for many years roamed around the smaller stables, with similar success to my own. In the last five years he has been recognised for the good jockey he is. In 1973 Fred Winter heard that all was not well between Willie and his trainer David Gandolfo, and said to me that he would be good enough for him if Willie was ever without

E

a job. Although the master of Uplands put up with me for so long, his choice of outside jockeys is of the highest order. Willie is good at every facet of the riding game, but unfortunately his financial rewards will be slender compared with his counterparts in any other sport.

A similar sort of chap to Willie is Ken White, a proud native of Upton-on-Severn who sports a broad Worcestershire brogue. In the early years he rode for the late Jack Yeomans at Upton-on-Severn and, although getting his full quota of winners, was not recognised as a leading jockey. Jack Yeomans liked to travel to Perth or any other far-off meeting where he could win races. This resulted in Ken White being overlooked by the bigger trainers, many of whom would have benefited from his services. To become fashionable a jockey needs to ride winners at the big southern tracks, where he is hailed by the racing scribes and implanted in other trainers' brains.

Unlike football, where first division scouts continually look for young talented players in the lower divisions, racing folk tend to associate jockeys with the type of horse they ride. After Jack Yeomans died, Fred Rimell took Ken on as second jockey and immediately his talents were acknowledged—not because his riding had improved, which it didn't need to, but because his mounts were of better quality: — 'Good horses make good jockeys'.

Ken has never returned to the weighing room cursing some idiot for bad riding: a smile and good advice would be his remedy. But let no man take him for a fool, or think him soft. He gives no quarter and asks none from the moment the race starts, and is certainly nobody's fool.

After Lanzarote defeated Comedy of Errors in the Champion Hurdle the two horses met at Cheltenham early the next season with victory going to Ken and Comedy of Errors by a length. When the two horses met for a decider at Leopardstown in the Irish Hospitals' Sweeps Hurdle the stage was really set for a battle royal. Both parties travelled over together and were met by Fred Rimell's stud manager, Sue Francis, who took us all to the same hotel in Dublin where we ate heartily. I am still not quite sure whether there was no ulterior motive behind Fred Rimell's recommendation that I should try the oysters: at any event, Fred Winter immediately squashed that idea in case they did not agree with me and would leave him without a jockey for the next day.

We went to the track together the morning of the race and we even worked the horses together for their final pipe opener. On returning to the hotel we breakfasted together before each party retreated to finalise plans for the match to come. I had a pacemaker to make the early running, leaving Ken to watch and wait for me to move. Three hurdles from home I swept past my pacemaker on his outside, telling his jockey to come off the rails and leave enough of a gap for Ken to bring 'Comedy' through, and when he was half way through, to shut the gap.

This was professionalism, not foul riding. Ken wisely refused the inside passage and followed my own tracks. He joined me at the last hurdle to go on for a length victory, a repeat of the previous meeting. As I have said he is a really nice guy but nobody's fool.

Probably the jockey recognised as the best all-rounder by the jockeys themselves is Jeff King. If pure ability was the test he would finish far higher in the jockeys' championship than he does. Jeff rides a race with a cool head, clear brain and superb judgement of pace, and he has one of the strongest finishes seen in modern-day steeplechasing. In some ways racing is now a branch of show business, but Jeff relies solely on his riding ability, steadfastly refusing to elaborate or gloss over a horse's performance. He has probably lost future winners by expressing his opinion with too much frankness and conviction.

When the demon drink is in us Jeff always attacked my attitudes to owners and trainers as bull or flannel, but I honestly think that when a horse runs badly a jockey must pick out the good points of the race so the owner can justify its existence to his wife and friends. At least, that is the best way with sporting owners; a man who wishes to back his horse must be told the stark truth, in case a flippant word causes him to invest good money on a poor animal. The trainer, in my opinion should be told how bad a horse is so that he can then put it to the owner himself.

Jeff has been race riding since he left school and hates the driving to meetings so when it's his turn the lads go in his car, but with Jeff in the passenger seat. To those who know him well he reveals a soft centre. He possesses a quick wit, will go anywhere for charity and is a good family man. Those who don't know him well should beware—he does not suffer fools gladly!

There is no class distinction in the changing room. All jockeys are equal, although there are three distinct professional groups. The biggest group consists of the annual influx of aspiring jockeys, most of whom vanish from the scene quite quickly. They are welcomed and advised by their senior counterparts. The middle group are young lads who survive the first year and visit the winner's enclosure spasmodically for the next eight years or so before finally deciding that the love of the game no longer compensates for the lack of money.

The last, and very much the smallest, group consists of the riders who have stood the test of time and the inescapable injuries and who command a salary big enough to live on.

The amateur riders are treated as if they were 'one of the boys' with rank or title meaning nothing. Away from the racecourse a gentleman rider may control a business empire and would normally be unreachable by a jockey. On the track, facing the same hazards and racing for the same prize, no rank is pulled. This may not be strictly true in the case of a woolly headed playboy, who having failed to justify a place in his family firm, turns his favours to racing. Those men, of course, are a tiny minority and if they appear to be a danger they are told quite firmly to get on the outside of the field at the rear.

At one time certain amateurs were being used purely because they rode for nothing, taking the bread from the mouths of professionals, but this is no longer so. Nowadays when an amateur has ridden in seventy-five races against professionals a fee is charged for his use, each time he rides in a professionals' race, the fee going into the Jockey Club's Joint Administration Fund. He may still ride for no charge in a Hunter Chase or Amateur Riders Race, which removes the bone of contention.

Of the senior amateur riders today Lord Oaksey and Dick Saunders would hold their own in the professional ranks if they were younger and in need of a job. Many of our top jockeys have started as gentlemen riders, the ones that spring to mind being Tommy Stack, Graham Thorner, Stan Mellor, Terry Biddlecombe, Bob Davies, Dick Francis, Tim Brookshaw and Bill Smith. All have been champion professional jockeys except Bill, who holds Fulke Walwyn's job and is the Royal Jockey under National Hunt Rules.

I recently heard a man criticise a jockey for blowing excessively at the end of a race. He said the rider should be fit enough to ride a finish without being out of breath. His theory does not hold water. At the start of each season it took me about twenty races before my wind was satisfactory, and I don't smoke. I would run for miles, play tennis, ride at exercise every day and swim, but only race riding would put the finishing touches to my wind. If you were to stand at the finish of the men's one hundred metres sprint in Montreal the winner would be breathless. Why should a jockey be fitter? At least signs of exhaustion means your man has put some effort into his work.

Of the few jockeys I have mentioned the common denominator is their strength of character. One man who possesses a mixture of all their attributes is my successor at Fred Winter's yard, Johnny Francome. In my opinion Johnny will be the next great Jockey—Josh Gifford and, before him, Fred Winter, being the last greats. His early show jumping career polished his eye for a jump. If you watch him during a race, you will see the minimum of effort from both parties because he organises his mount long before the obstacle is reached : valuable energy is saved for the winning end of the race. He is now the most stylish jockey to watch and has a far better than average brain. His finish, without being vigorous is very effective. And although he has had a lot of success he is still a hungry jockey. John has put every penny he has earned so far into bricks and mortar, denying himself any luxuries whatsoever. His thinking is on a par with Graham Thorner's; both men hold a great affection for money, but in no way are they mean with it, just careful. John and Graham are the new breed of jockey who realises that money does not flow eternally and that a jockey's career is a short one.

17   *Pendil*

My association with Pendil has been an extremely happy one, even though I blame myself for causing him to be the best Gold Cup horse never to win it. At the time of writing he is training for a third bid at the title and by publication date we will know whether third time is lucky.

Having thrilled me so much during the schooling session you can imagine my feelings as I drove from Lambourn to Cheltenham for Pendil's steeplechase debut. In my mind I rode the race over and over again, each time with the same result. The only way that Pendil could be beaten was by Lady Luck playing her hand once again. He is not made like a typical chaser, being of slight build behind the saddle and having lean hind quarters, but he possesses several attributes that the majority of racehorses lack. Whatever gait he uses he immediately gives the impression that he is an athelete. His walk is spritely, and has a gliding motion; his trot is springy, each stride covering half as much ground again as most other horses. Pendil's canter reverts to the glide; and his gallop is exhilarating.

Entering the parade ring he looked far from the machine he is, with his coat sticking up in the cold January wind and sporting a woolly head. Pendil mildly objects to being clipped at all and refuses to allow one hair from his head to be touched. This may be something to do with the pair of three-quarter inch horns that sprout from his forehead between his ears and eyes.

After the normal pre-race chit chat between trainer, jockey and the owners, a bell is rung as a signal to the jockeys to get mounted. As Fred Winter checked the girth straps and protective boots on his legs, Pendil's heart beat increased with excitement. He kicked out—from well being, not malice—and a slight sweat broke out on his neck. It had been nine months since he last ran in the Schweppes Hurdle, where he had contracted his leg trouble. Even so the procedure had not been forgotten. He knew that once the girths were tightened things started to happen.

The Guv'nor legged me into the saddle, wishing me luck before adding his usual parting phrase : 'Look after him and yourself'. As Vince Brooks led us around the crowded parade ring giving me his own set of instructions, eager racegoers made their comments; . . . 'Doesn't look like a chaser' . . . 'Must have been well schooled' . . . 'Wonder if that leg will stand up to a race'. A final 'Good Luck' from Vince and I was on my own.

Pendil ground his teeth making my nerve ends tingle. Eager to get on with it he broke into a canter the moment his feet felt turf beneath them. As we cantered to the start Pendil took a really strong hold of his bit, responding eventually to my soft-spoken patter—'Easy son, there's a long way to go'; 'Whoa boy, settle down'. Intelligent horses will listen to the tones of a rider's voice which has much more effect than brute force ever does.

I showed Pendil the first fence—which he thought was the office to jump it. Surging forward two strides away, he forced me to pull him sharply around. The Starter's assistant checked the girths again, managing to tighten them after his canter to the start.

Stan Mellor said he was going to make the running, but with the bold Barry Brogan in the race I thought that impossible. Sure enough, as soon as the tapes went up, Barry was away like a scalded cat with Stan in hot pursuit and Jeff King tucked in behind them. As these were the fancied runners I was delighted to follow at a respectable distance, keeping an eye on their moves. The first fence approached, and Pendil launched himself into the air while the horses level with me took another full stride. Deftly flicking out his landing gear, he was away the second his hooves touched the turf, making rapid progress on the leading three.

Too many jumps like that would take me to the lead long before I wanted to be there, so talking softly and pulling hard on the reins I managed to drop back to almost last position. Each fence was taken in his stride, never once faltering, never once doubting his own capability. As the race quickened into a headlong dash down that famous Cheltenham hill I could not restrain him any longer, and it would have been wrong of me to continue disappointing him. When I released a slight amount of rein the response was electrifying. Pendil surged forward, passing five horses at the one fence. It was the very fence where as a boy, many years before, I had watched crouched out of sight on my stolen day's racing.

There were just three horses in front of me then and it took only two of Pendil's enormous strides to settle the issue. Once in front with the running rail to lend support Pendil raced clear to fly the last fence as he had done the first and win easing up by fifteen lengths. Pendil was quite fresh when he entered the winners enclosure to a deafening reception: the racing enthusiasts all realised that they had witnessed a top class performance. The noise made him stop, look around and put his ears back in alarm until he received a reassuring pat from his owners, the pretty Mrs Swallow and her delightful mother, Mrs Corbett.

It is said that horses know when they have won a race and I am sure that they do. They must gather something from the kisses and affection that are showered upon them by all concerned. The losers always get a pat or two but without the heartfelt feeling that is reserved for the victor.

Fred Winter is one of the finest men that I have known and although he shows it in many ways, his attitude to the result of a race reveals his character. He greeted Pendil and myself quietly with a pat for each; an extra squeeze showed just *how* pleased he really was. The same attitude is shown in defeat—a pat and a few soothing words. He never explains a failure to the owners before waiting for the jockey to give his explanation first. To those who know him well, a twinkle in his eye gave away the excited feelings inside his head.

Pendil ran six times unbeaten that season, finishing by winning the Welsh Champion Chase at Chepstow by twelve lengths. Each race was won with the same tactics, behind early on in the race and delivering a devastating challenge as late as possible. A Land-Rover was beside the runners at Chepstow on the inside of the course. It clocked Pendil racing at 41 mph over the hundred yards when he actually raced past the other runners.

His second season over fences brought wins in major sponsored races and in the King George VI Gold Cup at Kempton Park on Boxing Day. This is the premier trial for the hallowed Cheltenham Gold Cup the following March. At Christmas The Dikler was still ante-post favourite for the Cheltenham race. Pendil disposed of that by beating him easily. So, after two more races, one run over two miles rather than the three and a quarter miles of the forthcoming title fight, Pendil was ready to take on the best England and Ireland could muster. In the two miles race among the rivals that he swallowed whole were none other than Tingle Creek and Inkslinger, the best jumpers in America at that time.

The stage was set for Pendil to take his rightful crown as he had beaten every horse in the race at some time or other. The percentage of the prize money to come was not important to me: I was after the prestige of the biggest race to be fought for at my home track. Pendil was being hailed as a second Arkle by nearly everyone on the racecourse. There was no apparent weakness in his make-up, except perhaps his stamina. The best two-milers had bowed to his superiority and he had beaten the best three-milers around Kempton's easy three mile circuit. That was easy work, because the track is completely flat and does not sap a horse's stamina to the same degree as Cheltenham's long uphill finish. But both Fred Winter and myself were confident that Pendil did not lack for stamina, or for anything else.

On the day of the 1973 Gold Cup I slept deeply while my

wife Jenny drove the thirty-six miles to Cheltenham. I awoke with a start just as we swept over the hill behind the race-course, tingling with excitement and ready for the fray. For thirteen years my aim had been to win Cheltenham Gold Cup and now I had my chance. I was, of course, used to big races by that time, but this was more than just a big race. Mrs Swallow and Mrs Corbett were visibly nervous in the parade ring together with Fred Winter, Vince Brooks and myself. The fact that we looked to be a certainty increased the pressure until none of us dared think about the race and we just made polite small talk for what seemed like an age. At last the mounting bell rang and it was time to start work. A final 'Good luck' from the owners, a pat on the boot from the Guv'nor, which said far more than words, and a choked 'Safe keeping' from a pale Vince Brooks saw me off. It was out of their hands now. Their work was done and it was up to Pendil and me.

No surprise tactics were needed as The Dikler had a pace-maker in the shape of Charlie Potheen, trained by Fulke Walwyn, a front runner on whom I had won the Hennessey Gold Cup earlier that season. He would ensure a fast-run race, enabling The Dikler to settle down and also testing Pendil's stamina to the full. As expected 'Charlie' was pushed into a definite lead with Clever Scot his nearest rival. I was ice-cool, thinking, solely about the job in hand but completely without warning Clever Scot made an uncharacteristic jumping error and paid the penalty. I had to quickly snatch Pendil's head round, hoping his body would follow to avoid the prostrate horse, which luckily it did. Disaster had been only inches away with the race only half over. Pendil was now roused and it took a deal of persuasion to get him to settle at the rear of the field. As in his first novice chase the downhill run took us close to the leaders, with a big jump at the third last fence taking Pendil to the front.

'Charlie' was quickly tiring, and this had the effect of stopping his stable mate, The Dikler, from getting a clear run. As he dropped back 'Charlie' took The Dikler with him, while Pendil sped towards the penultimate fence with a three length lead and full of running. A truly magnificent leap by Pendil at that fence must have clinched the result in most viewers' eyes. But never has the old adage that 'a horse has not won until it passes the winning post' been so true! Going to the last fence I could see my striding was not right for a 'long one' so, holding Pendil's head, I allowed him to jump normally. The entire crowd was silent as we soared over the fence, but erupted into hysterical shouting when we landed safely on the bright green strip of turf.

I started to urge Pendil away from the last fence towards the distant winning post, and for fifty yards he responded magnificently until we were crossing a junction in the track. Then the whole race suddenly became a nightmare. Jockeys are used to the unusual and ready for any emergency. I knew of Pendil's habit of idling when he thought he had won a race but was unprepared for what took place in the next four seconds, seconds that took years off my life.

I could not believe it was happening. His body tensed as we raced between the tightly packed crowd, most of whom were shouting and throwing hats into the air. His tightened muscles then completely froze, causing his head to come upwards and back towards my face as if he was frightened. His momentum kept him going, but at a much reduced speed. All my efforts to force him back to reality were in vain until he felt The Dikler's presence at his quarters; but then it was too late to save us. Even though Pendil rallied to fight for the lead, the winning post came a second too soon. We flashed across the line together with the next stride taking Pendil to the front, but I did not need to wait for the photo-finish to be developed to know our fate : the Gold Cup was not ours.

It is my honest opinion that had I held Pendil back for a later challenge, or even had The Dikler's first challenge not been stopped by Charlie Potheen, we would have won the Gold Cup by two or three lengths. Pendil's sequence of eleven wins had been broken by a short head.

The next season, 1973–74, he won his first four races including the Massey Ferguson Gold Cup and his second King George VI Chase. Cheltenham was the venue for the return match between Pendil and The Dikler, with Helmsman receiving two and a half stones and Tingle Creek thrown in for good measure. I allowed Pendil to be prominent this time, because Tingle Creek was sure to make it a strong gallop. The race went according to plan with The Dikler never showing his nose and Tingle Creek folding up half a mile from home. This left Helmsman and Pendil to come off the last bend neck and neck, both full of running. I was aware that every pound of the two and a half stones Pendil had to concede to his rival would count double up the finishing-climb to the post so I decided to use Pendil's ace card, his great heart.

It was my opinion that Helmsman was a slightly moody character and that my best chance of victory was to disappoint him. Approaching the last jump I asked Pendil to take off fully two strides before the fence and without hesitation he obeyed. This action had the desired effect with Helmsman losing the upper hand and the race. The Dikler ran on to be third, beaten twenty-one and a half lengths, but it did not change the fact that his name had been inscribed on the Cheltenham Gold Cup, not ours.

We next met on Boxing Day in the King George VI Chase at Kempton with much the same result. This time Pendil finished thirty-two lengths in front of his rival.

Finally Gold Cup day came round once again with the usual runners, plus Captain Christy and High Ken, a horse just out of the novice stage and unreliable at his obstacles. After weighing out I was told there had been a telephone threat the previous day that Pendil would be shot before he reached the winning post. Fred Winter gave express orders that I should not be told because of the undue pressure it would put on me, but it made litle difference to my state of mind. A jockey forgets everything else the moment the tapes go up and even severe pain vanishes when the race is on.

Before Vince Brookes let me loose he asked me to get the horse withdrawn at the start rather than risk Pendil's life. If it was a hoax it was in poor taste for Vince had sat on guard the whole of the previous night and was mentally and physically worn out. The race was run much the same as the previous year with Charlie Potheen cutting out the early pace and this time Inkslinger being the half-way faller. Pendil jumped his prostrate body and I sighed with relief. As we turned down the hill a new leader in the shape of High Ken took over from Charlie Potheen with the Queen Mother's Game Spirit, ridden by Terry Biddlecombe, in second place.

Pendil pulled me alongside Terry who said 'Don't hem me in behind that sod, he doesn't jump very well'. I was too close to the leader too soon so I tried to ease Pendil back, but he was absolutely running away, he resisted my attempts. Fate played its hand as the downhill fence loomed up. Terry was on my inside, but I had an escape route on the outside of High Ken. As we approached the fence both Captain Christy and The Dikler came up on my outside closing the gap which could have been my saviour. The inevitable happened. High Ken made his first mistake of the race and crashed to the ground, leaving Pendil nowhere to land.

The result was the same as if a trip wire had been placed across the course. Pendil's legs were snatched from under him, throwing both of us to the ground. I sat up to see Pendil on his feet, looking bewildered with his ears flat back. He had never fallen in his life and then, having put in yet another superb jump, had experienced the world looking upside down. He waited for a brief second before setting off in vain pursuit of the distant runners, leaving me to my thoughts.

It was only yards away from the very spot where sixteen years earlier I had played truant to watch with awe racing horses and their gallant riders. My thoughts were on childhood when Bob Davies, High Ken's jockey brought me back to reality with a jolt. Facing the disappointed connections was the hardest thing I have ever had to do probably, largely they are all such nice people. I learned later that Mrs Swallow thought at first Pendil had been shot. One cannot imagine the agony she must have gone through at that time.

After this second blow, Pendil resumed his winning ways in the 1974–75 season. The jockeys all took to making slow paces, forcing me to make all of the running and hoping that Pendil would get bored with the job. He had to struggle but he won his next three races. The second of these was at Sandown Park when a huge crowd had gathered to see Pendil challenge Tingle Creek again, this time over the minimum distance, two miles.

From my position, several lengths behind Tingle Creek down the whole length of the back straight, it was a joy to watch him stand off at every fence. For the people in the stands it must have been an exhibition of a lifetime. Everytime Tingle produced a prodigious leap Pendil did the same. Jumping is the name of the game, and jumping is what they did.

Switching to challenge on Tingle Creek's outside as we raced to the last fence I knew I would win, but it was not going to be easy. Both horses flew it as one while the crowd went mad with delight, each shouting for his favourite. Pendil won by one and a half lengths and received a tumultuous reception when he entered the winner's enclosure. All that is good about steeplechasing was revealed when the loser received the same reception from the crowd. They had witnessed a great battle and showed their appreciation.

Sadly, my last season as Pendil's partner ended with three defeats. Captain Christy, in one of his better moods, ended our monopoly in the King George VI Chase and Shock Result provided just that at Newbury beating Pendil—at 25–1—by two lengths with Bula ten lengths back in fourth place. Our last racecourse appearance together was at Kempton. Going to the last fence Pendil's stride shortened and he almost stopped to jump it, completely out of character. Both Cuckholder and Highland Seal finished in front of us, something which had never happened before in twenty-three races over fences. As I approached the line the awful truth became apparent—

Pendil was lame. He limped back to the enclosure, not understanding why he was in pain or why he was in the berth
reserved for the third horse. He was taken out of the Cheltenham Gold Cup, only three weeks away and for which he had
been installed as firm favourite for the third year running.
Thanks to the wealth of talent in Fred Winter's yard I still
was able to ride Soothsayer into second spot in the Gold Cup
but the special meaning the race had for me disappeared
when Pendil was taken out.

18   A bitter pill to swallow

Pendil's short head defeat by The Dikler was the first of three body blows within the space of twenty-one days. Two weeks after the Gold Cup I rode Crisp in the Grand National, a race for which he was equal favourite with Red Rum. His win in the 1972 Two Mile Champion Chase had confirmed that despite his nine years his speed had not waned, which he reasserted a year later with a record breaking two and a half miles chase victory at Newbury. His owner, Sir Chester Manifold, bowed to our wishes and allowed Crisp to be entered for the Grand National on the reasoning that a horse that does not get three miles can sometimes stay the four and a half miles at Aintree.

It was decided that a tilt at a second Two Mile Champion Chase a fortnight before Aintree would provide a handsome prize without too much strain on Crisp's fitness. He started at odds on for the Champion Chase, but he over-reacted to my settling tactics and was beaten two and three quarter lengths by Inkslinger. I thought that his lack-lustre performance was due to my covering him up instead of using his forceful front running capabilities. This posed the problem of what to do at Aintree. Should we use his jumping and risk his unproved stamina, or should we hold him back, risking jumping behind slower horses? Fred Winter told me to be handy on the inside of the track where the jumps are bigger, but fewer people choose to go. The ground was firm which would favour both us and our market rival, Red Rum. The two horses were the medium of huge gambles from regular punters which spread to housewives all over the country, and they started inseparable at the odds of 9–1.

A good sweat in the Southport Turkish Baths, supported by several glasses of champagne, was my traditional start to Grand National day, handed down over the years from the senior jockeys. The great mystery of the Grand National and the chance to have a bumper pay day causes butterflies, not fear, in the stomach of every jockey taking part. On arrival at the course the telegram rack was always my first stop to see which absent friends had remembered me. The ancient changing room provides scarcely any space for every jockey taking part, with the valets treading on everybody's toes as they scuttle about their business. Chatty people become quiet, quiet ones can't stop talking, a non-smoker will come in with a pipe belching out clouds of smoke and Lord Oaksey carries two bags of glucose and orange quarters which he swallows alternately.

For several decades the late Lord Sefton gave a fatherly talk to all the jockeys shortly before the bell to signal the jockeys exit. This chore has been taken over by Lord Leverhulme, who must have found Lord Sefton's script. On the way to the parade ring many hands are shaken and messages of good luck given freely almost as if the jockey is expected to disappear in a puff of smoke. Once in the paddock every jockey finds a reason for fancying his horse's chance even though in the cold light of reality half of them have none.

Crisp looked at peak fitness when stripped of his light paddock rug but, knowing that a race was imminent when this happened, started to sweat a little from excitement. There is always an air of happiness and anticipation at this point. I have a quick verbal exchange with that smiling red-headed giant 'Ginger' McCain.

'Don't know why you bothered to bring that sprint-bred pony,' I said as I passed his party.

'Well, you lot had the cheek to bring your overfed kangaroo,' he replied. The parade down the track takes ten minutes in which time the younger horses jog sideways not being used to the huge crowd and all the noise they make while the older participants walk with a somewhat bored air. Chippy Chape,

Crisp's lad, doesn't trust the overworked Starter's assistant so he checked the girths himself before fading from sight. As we milled around at the start I asked Willie Shoemark what his plans were. He replied that he was going to make the running on the outside. That suited me. I would get a lead from him, but we would be on opposite sides of the track. When the starter calls the jockeys into line an immediate flush raced right through the body. The roar, 'They're off,' has such force that any jockey not wanting to be up with the leaders has no choice as his horse leaps forward, surprised by the sudden shout.

I urged Crisp into immediate action tight to the inside rails where only the better jumpers dare to go. It is a fair run to the first fence, with most riders trying to get a good look at it. Crisp saw the first fence, took a hold of his bit and accelerated towards it. If Fred Winter had waved a thousand pound note in front of me there was no way I would have been able to stop for it. I checked Crisp's stride the moment he landed.

To my surprise he responded for twenty yards or so before catching sight of the next fence, going at it as if he wanted to eat it. I realised that I would unbalance him if we fought too much so I just kept hold of his head until inside the massive wings of the fence where I gave him the office to jump. It was obvious that until the edge had gone off him he was going to have the upper hand going into a fence, making it imperative that I had control on landing. Had he not responded, his headlong dash from fence to fence would have resulted in utter exhaustion after a mile and a half.

The third fence at Aintree is greatly underestimated in my opinion. It is as big as 'The Chair' and comes after two small fences, catching the cocky horse or rider by surprise. I fell twice at this fence and felt wonderful as Crisp sailed over it with utter contempt. He had shown me his Aintree potential and with it instilled all the confidence I needed to be as brave as him. It is vital that both horse and rider be on a par with each other.

Three fences later, a little red flag with a white letter B inserted, indicated that we were approaching Beecher's Brook. I looked across the track to Willie Shoemark on Grey Sombrero and shouted, 'This is it Willie, here's the big one,' Willie started to reply but then decided to concentrate on his approach to it instead. Crisp again accelerated, meeting it just right, powered into the air and soared over the top. His jump took him further away from the fence than I had ever been before which made the enormous drop on landing seem like eternity. It was like stepping into the unknown, expecting your legs to be snatched away any second. He did not peck on landing as most horses do to counter balance their speed and surprise at finding no ground to land on at the normal height.

The first six fences at Aintree are jumped in a straight line before turning left-handed to the smallest fence on the course. This poses yet another problem to horses. Having just got over the shock of Beecher's big drop they expect another but the ground this time comes up to meet them with its green arms ready to trip up the uninitiated. My passage round the inner was now beginning to tell, for without increasing my speed I had gone several lengths clear of Grey Sombrero.

The track at the Canal Turn runs away at right angles to the fence making it necessary to jump across it rather than straight. With no other horses around, Crisp was able to do my bidding and a superb cross jump, causing my boot to brush the wing, enabled our lead to be increased again. The distant stands, a murky group of buildings, grew with each fast calculated leap Crisp made until approaching the fifteenth fence the enormity of 'The Chair' fence blotted out everything else. It has a yawning ditch on the take-off side of a five foot six inch thorn fence with the ground slightly raised on the landing side, ready to trip up any unbalanced horse. Crisp flicked the top of the fence as if to test its might and without more ado headed for the water.

Grey Sombrero, the nearest rival, was already some fifteen lengths back, and fell at this point leaving Crisp fully twenty-five lengths clear of the pack. One circuit had been completed without mishap and we held a clear lead. The crowd no doubt had divided opinions as to the merits of being so far clear. Could the two-miler Crisp keep up this gallop for another two and a quarter miles? Or, alternatively, it was thought that he was so far clear he could not be caught. Brian Fletcher on Red Rum decided to get a closer look at us and started to work hard in pursuit. For the last ten fences the noise of my pursuers had been diminishing until now I was alone. It was quite eerie.

As we jumped our way down to Beecher's second time, the relics of the first circuit were to be seen everywhere. Great holes in some of the fences told tales of heavy falls and shattered dreams. A bridle that had been wrenched off a horse's head as he trod on the dangling reins when he tried to get up on his feet, lay broken on the grass. Horseless jockeys leaned on the rails, their chance of glory gone for another year. On the approach to Beecher's David Nicholson, who had been reunited with Highland Seal said, 'You are well clear, kick on. Good Luck'. I had no intention of kicking on at that point—there was still a long way to go. Crisp flew Beecher's as if it was a hurdle. The commentary at that point by Michael O'Hehir told me that my nearest rival was Red Rum, thirty lengths behind.

The Guv'nor's words of so many years before echoed in my head: 'You can't win if you don't get round.' I still had eight fences to jump and one and a half miles to gallop. Crisp was still moving well with his legs flicking out in front of him and his strength giving no signs of waning. Each of the next six jumps we took with precision until crossing the thirty yards of cinders covering the Melling road I felt Crisp's action change slightly.

'Just two fences to go, keep hold of his head, keep him balanced,' I said to myself. Though tiring, Crisp jumped the penultimate fence well and having given him a breather I now drove him towards the last obstacle between us and victory in the world's greatest steeplechase. As I pushed and urged Crisp on I caught sounds of a pursuer. The first sound I heard was the flapping of nostrils as he forced each breath out of his lungs, joined by the drumming of hoofs on the firm ground.

Crisp popped over the last which was quite knocked about from the first time round, but no longer had the strength to shoot away from it. Instead his tired limbs carried his twelve stone burden towards the winning post at only half his previous speed.

The run-in between the last fence and victory was the longest and most agonising four hundred and ninety-four yards I will ever have to travel. My aching limbs had now given their best and every breath I snatched scalded my wind-pipe as if it was boiling water. No longer was Crisp's action light and forward, it was now laboured and sideways as if he was drunk. The tell-tale noises were close, but so was the winning post—or was it? It almost seemed as if it was moving further away with each stride.

With only fifteen yards to go Crisp tightened as he felt Red Rum's presence but it was his dying effort and only lasted for a second. Two strides away from the post Red Rum's head forged past my gallant partner to snatch victory from our grasp.

Chippy Chape was white as a ghost, his mind exhausted from emotions so deep that he could not utter a word until we reached the enclosure reserved for the second horse. When Crisp and I were fighting for our breath, Chippy hardly dared breathe at all in case he missed anything. I was overcome with a new sensation. I was tingling with the deep thrills and emotions that my mind and body had experienced during the last hectic nine minutes. In fact the time of the race was 9 mins. 1.9 secs. which broke Golden Miller's record for the race by no less than nineteen seconds—a record that had stood for thirty-nine years.

Fred Winter, watching the race with Sir Chester Manifold did not speak a single word throughout the race until Crisp jumped the second last fence when he said, 'I'm afraid Sir Chester, we are going to be beaten.' In giving 25 lb. in weight to Red Rum, Crisp had lost nothing in defeat and I had had an experience that will last me to my grave.

So, within the space of a fortnight I had been beaten a short head in the Gold Cup and three-quarters of a length in the Grand National. It was difficult to imagine that there was worse to come, but seven days later the worst thing of all was to happen.

Killiney was a horse with unbounded potential, who had won his only nine steeplechases. Mr and Mrs Rex Boucher had the champion they set out to find with only their second horse. Killiney had won six hurdles races as well as his nine chases, beating every novice that England and Ireland could produce. He jumped superbly, pulverising the opposition by halfway in his races. His greatest triumph came just three weeks before his death: a smooth win in the Champion Novice's Chase at Cheltenham. Then, in a four horse field at Ascot, Killiney looked as if he just needed to stay in third gear to land his tenth consecutive steeplechase. Not wishing to give him a hard race, I restrained him more than usual, allowing him to be upsides in front rather than twenty lengths clear of the rest at halfway.

We turned away from the packed stands to start on the final circuit, skipping over a plain fence to approach the downhill open ditch where Killiney was right for one of his enormous jumps. As he started to rise I went with him but then he changed his mind and tried to put a short stride in before the fence. His speed and size did not allow this to happen and he 'put down' right into the open ditch itself. I was catapulted out of the saddle for some way before landing on my head, suffering severe concussion and dislocating a shoulder. I dimly remember my old pal Killiney standing still while I was carried to the ambulance. It was the last time I ever saw him. He had broken his shoulder, and had to be destroyed.

Defeat can always be turned to victory another day, but death is final. I am not very sentimental about many things, or indeed humans. But to this day the memory of Killiney hurts badly.

19 *Fit to ride*

My career was extremely spasmodic to begin with, but it gathered strength to end with five successful years. All along the line I was fortunate enough to meet people who, in varying degrees, gave me a helping hand.

Along with Fred Winter no one has helped me more than Lord Cadogan, one of the best men I have dealt with. I first came to know him when I rode for Major Bewicke, where he was the principal owner, and when they split up he left five horses in the south for me to ride in order that I would not lose through their affairs. His friendship changed my life more than my uneducated hand can possibly do justice to, and in his case as in so many others I hope that the end of my riding career will not mean the end of the friendships that have grown with me. For any professional sportsman the decision to retire is like naming the day that you will marry—both are inevitable, but it is a case of when and how.

The odds were stacked heavily in favour of my riding for several seasons more, but I plumped instead for the long term. My steeplechasing days were both past and present, but my wife and two sons will want to eat long after the horses have stopped winning for me.

Pendil, Lanzarote, Crisp and Floating Pound could have provided my living for some years, but not indefinitely. I felt as if I were deserting my equine friends, but then Johnny Francome's capable hands and cool head will be steering them safely to victory.

At last I decided that the time had come to retire. My weight was as severe a problem as ever, and a new career was opening up: after a chance beginning, commenting on the

1974 Whitbread Gold Cup, the BBC had sought my services for the television.

Although I knew how to do the deed I put it off for six days in a row, finally blurting my intentions out to the Guv'nor, not at all as coolly as I had rehearsed. Fred Winter said nothing for a long time, and then said, 'I had hoped you would ride a little longer, but you know your own mind.' This great man and trainer never speaks without first thinking the situation over from both sides and his one sentence reassured me that I had done the right thing.

With a week of the season left, the scene was set and although I rode on four days that last week, I did not really accept the finality of it all until I woke on the last morning. I went to the stables to say good-bye to the boys and the horses with whom I had shared so much drama—the deep depressions when winners just would not come, and also those days when the air rang with cheers and congratulations for another winner.

The road to Stratford-on-Avon seemed longer than ever before, but I knew when I arrived that it was the begining of the end. To give up when the fences seem bigger and the open ditches wider would be easy, but when your heart is still in the game to stop is both hard and sad. The usual jolly faces and friendly retorts from the gatemen, paper sellers, punters, friends and even touts and spivs only helped to make the realisation of my last ride stick.

On entering the Weighing Room I showed my medical record book. The last line read 'Fit to ride' and above that statement of fact was written the evidence in red writing of my falls, breaks, cracks, dislocations and periods of concussion. Indeed I am a lucky man to finish after riding 7,400 miles on the racecourse over some 85,000 jumps. Fit to ride. Through the swing doors into the changing room where the buzz of chatter is louder than at any Woman's Institute, jokes are bandied around, the heroes of the season are being congratulated, the others recalling their bad luck, a few injured jockeys eager to start a fresh season and me, now quite numb, because in one hour's time, I will leave this room and its inmates never to be allowed there again.

I rode St Swithin to finish a distant sixth—not the fairy-tale ending I had hoped for. But as I left the course there were many friends and only a few enemies to wish me luck in my new career. Suddenly I felt five years younger, I was starting on a new advanture into the world of television, and if I can meet its challenge I look forward to many years on the fringe of steeplechasing and my second and last retirement when I draw the old age pension.